A Guide to
Understanding
Essential Biblical
Themes

GOD AND HIS WAYS

BIBLE
MODULAR
SERIES

Bob Jones University Press, Greenville, South Carolina 29614

This textbook was written by members of the faculty and staff of Bob Jones University. Standing for the "old-time-religion" and the absolute authority of the Bible since 1927, Bob Jones University is the world's leading Fundamentalist Christian university. The staff of the University is devoted to educating Christian men and women to be servants of Jesus Christ in all walks of life.

Providing unparalleled academic excellence, Bob Jones University prepares its students through its offering of over one hundred majors, while its fervent spiritual emphasis prepares their minds and hearts for service and devotion to the Lord Jesus Christ.

If you would like more information about the spiritual and academic opportunities available at Bob Jones University, please call **1-800-BJ-AND-ME** (1-800-252-6363). www.bju.edu

NOTE:

The fact that materials produced by other publishers may be referred to in this volume does not constitute an endorsement by Bob Jones University Press of the content or theological position of materials produced by such publishers. The position of Bob Jones University Press, and the University itself, is well known. Any references and ancillary materials are listed as an aid to the student or the teacher and in an attempt to maintain the accepted academic standards of the publishing industry.

God and His Ways

Bryan Smith, M.A.
Coart Ramey, M.A.

Project Editors: Tom Parr and Catherine Anderson
Designers: Noelle Snyder and Dan VanLeeuwen
Cover Design: John Bjerk and Elly Kalagayan
Composition: Jennifer Hearing and Rebecca G. Zollinger

ISBN 1-57924-618-4

15 14 13 12 11 10 9 8 7 6 5 4 3 2

Photograph Credits

The following agencies and individuals have furnished materials to meet the photographic needs of this textbook. We wish to express our gratitude to them for their important contribution.

©1999-2001 www.arttoday.com
Bill and Janie McCauley
Bob Jones University Collection
Burke Library, Union Theological Seminary
Christian & Missionary Alliance (C&MA)
Corel Corporation
Digital Stock
J. B. Williams
Library of Congress
Medison 3D Images
National Aeronautics and Space Administration (NASA)
PhotoDisc, Inc.
Princeton Theological Seminary

Introduction Page
©1999-2001 www.arttoday.com iv; The Archives Collection of the Library of the Princeton Theological Seminary x

Chapter 1
Courtesy of C&MA 3; Courtesy of J. B. Williams 12 (both); *Isaiah's Lips Anointed with Fire* by Benjamin West, From the Bob Jones University Collection 15; ©1999-2001 www.arttoday.com 29

Chapter 2
Digital Stock 31; PhotoDisc, Inc. 39, 42, 43, 45; NASA 33; ©1999-2001 www.arttoday.com 34; Medison 3D Images 39; Library of Congress 45; Archives of the Burke Library, Union Theological Seminary in the City of New York 52

Chapter 3
Corel Corporation 69; PhotoDisc, Inc. 76

Chapter 6
Library of Congress 123; ©1999-2001 www.arttoday.com 131, 144; Courtesy of Bill and Janie McCauley 133; PhotoDisc, Inc. 141

CONTENTS

*T*heology?!

Why Study Theology?

I don't remember being nervous. Of course as an eighth grader, I was never completely comfortable talking with strangers about the gospel. But I knew the "Romans road" like the back of my hand, and I had knocked on dozens of doors in the past.

Knock, knock, knock.

"Yes. What do you want?"

"Hello, my name is Bryan Smith, and I'm from Faith Baptist Church." Within a minute I had asked the man at the door if he was certain he would be in heaven when he died.

"Well, I'm a Catholic," he said. "And I don't think that anyone can be certain about where he will be when he dies."

After explaining that the Bible says we can know that we're going to heaven, I asked if I could share with him what the Bible said about being saved. He agreed and soon we were working through Romans 3:23; 6:23; 5:8; and 10:13. Once we got to the last verse, I explained, "All God asks of you is that you call on the name of the Lord. If you do that, you will be saved."

"Pray, eh? Well then, I guess I am going to heaven. I pray every night."

Slam!

As I stared at the closed front door, I felt embarrassed and defeated. I was confident that this man was not born again, yet given the explanations of Scripture that I had presented, he had good reason to think he was.

In the years that followed, I often reflected on that incident, trying to figure out what had gone wrong that day on that front porch. In time I realized it was not simply that something "went wrong that day." The problem was much deeper. My understanding of what the Bible said about salvation was shallow. I knew enough to help some people but not enough to help that man. Through the experience I began to learn an important lesson: if I wanted to be an effective witness for Christ, I would need a broader and deeper knowledge of Bible doctrine and theology.

DOCTRINE THEOLOGY DOCTRINE THEOLOGY DOCTRINE THEOLOGY DOCTRINE THEOLOGY DOCTRINE THEOLOGY

This conclusion may seem strange to some people. After all, theology and doctrine have quite a stodgy reputation. "His preaching is very *doctrinal*." "That ministry focuses on teaching *theology*." To many people, such statements are simply a nice way of saying that a sermon is boring or irrelevant. Such a view, however, is tragically misguided. The word *doctrine* refers to a teaching that is systematically presented. When we systematically present a teaching from the Bible, it is called a biblical doctrine. *Theology* comes from two Greek words (*theos* and *logos*) that together mean "the study of God." Correctly understood, theological study is the most practical and relevant human pursuit. Through it, a person attempts to learn more about God by studying the teachings of the Bible systematically.

Far from being irrelevant, theology offers a rich reward to all those who study it. As I began to discover in the eighth grade, studying Bible doctrine enables a person to minister more effectively to others. Before leaving this world, Christ commanded His followers to make disciples of the nations by "teaching them to observe all things whatsoever I have commanded you" (Matt. 28:19-20). By identifying the essential teachings of the Lord and systematizing them into coherent discussions, theology makes the most important themes of the Bible readily accessible. As a believer studies theology, he becomes better equipped to share with others what the Bible says about God and His world. This study enables the believer to reason with lost people about the gospel, as Paul often did during his ministry (Acts 17:2). It also gives the Christian the skill necessary to establish other believers in the faith, so that they "be no more children, tossed to and fro, and carried about with every wind of doctrine" (Eph. 4:14).

Nevertheless, as rewarding as these benefits are, the personal benefit of studying theology is even greater. The student of theology enjoys the blessing of filling his mind with thoughts of God. Through the study he learns to view God, His world, and his own place in that world from a biblical perspective. This renewing perspective has the potential of changing the most personal aspects of his life. It can make him better able to read the Bible with profit, pray with confidence, and meditate with purpose. Such a study affects the believer's heart even more than it does his mind.

What Is Theology?

Since there are many ways to approach studying God and His relations to the world, the word *theology* has many different uses. It can refer to all the subjects in religious studies. Chief among these studies are four disciplines, each bearing the label "theology." **Biblical theology** limits itself to the explicit teaching of the Bible— what the Bible actually says. For example, a course in biblical theology may discuss the theological themes developed in Ezra, Micah, or Acts. **Historical theology** traces the development of theological thought throughout history, from the close of the New Testament canon to the present. Such studies may focus on the religious beliefs and teachings of Augustine, Martin Luther, or John Calvin. **Practical theology** focuses on teaching preachers how the theological content of the Scriptures should be applied to daily life. It addresses topics such as how to preach a sermon, how to organize a Sunday school program, how to conduct a worship service, and how to support missionary endeavors. **Systematic theology**, on the other hand, is that discipline that collects information regarding the essential themes found throughout the Bible and summarizes them in a coherent fashion. Its chief characteristics distinguishing it from biblical theology are drawing logical inferences from biblical statements and seeking contemporary applications from those statements. The central theme in this study is the Scripture's teaching about God Himself. This theme is also referred to as theology (often called **theology proper**).

DIFFERENT USES OF "THEOLOGY"

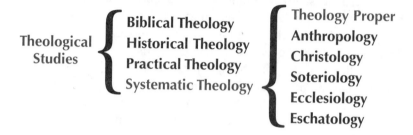

Theological Studies
{
Biblical Theology
Historical Theology
Practical Theology
Systematic Theology
}

{
Theology Proper
Anthropology
Christology
Soteriology
Ecclesiology
Eschatology
}

This course presents a survey of systematic theology. In our study we will examine what the Bible says about God (theology proper), man (anthropology), Christ (Christology), salvation (soteriology), and the church (ecclesiology). In each chapter we will collect the most important passages dealing with one of these themes. Then we will analyze those portions to determine what we are to believe regarding God and His ways.

How Should We Proceed?

A few years ago when I was attending a preaching conference, I met Dick. Just as I was sitting down, he introduced himself and asked me what I did for a living. When I told him that, among other things, I was pursuing an advanced degree in religious studies, he was more than a little offended. "So you think that in order to be prepared to serve God, you've got to have a doctorate?" I tried to answer him, but I soon learned that his question was rhetorical. For the next few minutes, Dick exhorted me about the importance of maintaining a right relationship with God. After the service he lectured me for thirty minutes on the dangers of academic pride. Dick was convinced that I was on the slippery slope to spiritual ruin simply because I was studying theology on an advanced level.

That unpleasant experience leads us to consider an important question. If theology is as biblical, practical, and relevant as I have said, why does it have a bad reputation with many sincere Christians? The problem lies not with the study itself. Theology has gained a bad reputation with some people because many students of theology approach their study with the wrong attitudes. If this course is to benefit you and those you will influence, you must approach it with the right attitudes.

Proceed with Humility

The student of theology often struggles to maintain a humble spirit. The flesh is amazingly adept at twisting a believer's desire for understanding and defending the truth into a desire for self-exaltation. Instead of growing into a more capable servant of God and man, he may become an obnoxious know-it-all. Yet the irony is that this sort of pride results from ignorance, not knowledge. As the apostle Paul warned, "If any man think that he knoweth any thing, he knoweth nothing yet as he ought to know" (I Cor. 8:2). The more we learn about God and His expectations for us, the more humility we should evidence.

This humility should manifest itself, first of all, in an *attitude of supplication*. Without God's special intervention, we cannot discover the true benefits of theology. The disciples never understood what the Bible taught about Christ until He "opened . . . their understanding, that they might understand the scriptures" (Luke 24:45). Certainly we are no better than those first-century followers. We must humbly go forward in this study with the prayer of the psalmist in our hearts and on our lips: "Open thou mine eyes, that I may behold wondrous things out of thy law" (Ps. 119:18).

Second, we should manifest our humility with an *attitude of submission*. We are not studying theology simply to broaden our knowledge. God does not reveal Himself to people to make them smart. He reveals Himself to change lives. The apostle Paul had been a theologian of sorts for many years before he met the Lord on the road to Damascus. He had sat at the feet of Gamaliel and was, in his own words, "taught according to the perfect manner of

At the dawn of the twentieth century, when theological liberals and conservatives clashed over the inspiration and authority of the Bible, Benjamin B. Warfield stood at the center of the fray, defending the Scriptures. Warfield was one of the most learned theologians of his day; nevertheless, theology to him was much more than books and arguments. The following exhortation that he once gave to theological students demonstrates that Warfield believed studying doctrine was a means of communing with God.

"Recruiting officers do not dispute whether it is better for soldiers to have a right leg or a left leg: soldiers should have both legs. Sometimes we hear it said that ten minutes on your knees will give you a truer, deeper, more operative knowledge of God than ten hours over your books. 'What!' is the appropriate response, 'than ten hours over your books, on your knees?' Why should you turn from God when you turn to your books, or feel that you must turn from your books in order to turn to God? . . . In your case there can be no 'either-or' here—either a student or a man of God. You must be both."

---

the law of the fathers" (Acts 22:3). Yet all of that learning was useless to him until his learning broke his will. The glorified Christ told him, "I am Jesus of Nazareth, whom thou persecutest" (Acts 22:8). Saul of Tarsus replied, "What shall I do, Lord?" (v. 10). Only then could Ananias say to Saul, "Thou shalt be [God's] witness unto all men of what thou hast seen and heard" (v. 15). Our study will be useless to us unless we mix it with the attitude of Saul: "What shall I do, Lord?"

Proceed with Praise

Systematic theology can be mentally demanding, and for this reason those who study it sometimes lose their focus and view the subject as just another academic burden. We, however, can avoid this harmful error if we will remember that examining God's revelation is a great privilege. In his letter to the Romans, Paul explains that God is angry with unbelievers because they have ignored His revelation found in nature. Rather than embracing God's unwritten message, they "glorified him not as God, neither were thankful" (Rom. 1:21). As students of theology, we enjoy a fuller revelation. We have God's written Word and enjoy the privilege of being guided by believers who have studied it in depth. This unusual privilege demands that we praise God by giving Him the two things that Paul says the unsaved have denied Him: *glory and thanksgiving.*

Are you thankful for the privilege of studying theology? The Lord was not obligated to reveal Himself to us, and certainly, if He had not revealed Himself, we never would have been able to know Him. The blessing of holding in our hands the sixty-six books of the Old and New Testaments is no small blessing. As Christ told His disciples, we who enjoy this full revelation have much to be thankful for: "Blessed are your eyes. . . . Many prophets and righteous men have desired to see those things which ye see, and have not seen them" (Matt. 13:16-17).

We also have an obligation to glorify God with our study. The more God reveals Himself to His creatures, the greater their obligation to glorify Him becomes. The winged creatures who stand in the presence of God beholding the full splendor of His glory are dedicated to one activity: "They rest not day and night, saying, Holy, holy, holy, Lord God Almighty, which was, and is, and is to come" (Rev. 4:8). If those who behold God's face should devote themselves to glorifying Him continually, can we legitimately suppose that our only obligation before God in this study is taking tests and quizzes?

Our study will at times be mentally challenging, but we should never think that it is just a mental pursuit. We are attempting to look through the doorway to the throne room of God, see past the lightnings and the sea of glass, and gaze on the One who was and is and is to come. By His grace our study will help us join the joyful song of the four and twenty elders.

Thou art worthy, o Lord, to receive glory & honour & power: for thou hast created all things, and for thy pleasure they are and were created.

CHAPTER ONE

Behold Your God!

1

Memory Verses: Exodus 34:6-7

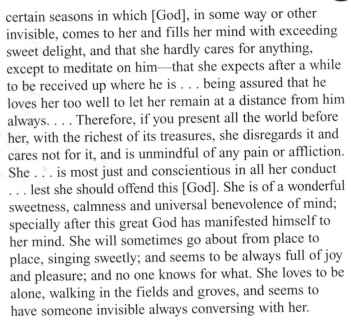

The flower of romance began to bloom in Jonathan's heart as he scrawled a note to himself in the flyleaf of one of his textbooks. In those lines he pondered the virtues of a certain "young lady in New Haven [Connecticut] who is beloved of that Great Being who made and rules the world." He wrote that he had heard she enjoyed

certain seasons in which [God], in some way or other invisible, comes to her and fills her mind with exceeding sweet delight, and that she hardly cares for anything, except to meditate on him—that she expects after a while to be received up where he is . . . being assured that he loves her too well to let her remain at a distance from him always. . . . Therefore, if you present all the world before her, with the richest of its treasures, she disregards it and cares not for it, and is unmindful of any pain or affliction. She . . . is most just and conscientious in all her conduct . . . lest she should offend this [God]. She is of a wonderful sweetness, calmness and universal benevolence of mind; specially after this great God has manifested himself to her mind. She will sometimes go about from place to place, singing sweetly; and seems to be always full of joy and pleasure; and no one knows for what. She loves to be alone, walking in the fields and groves, and seems to have someone invisible always conversing with her.

The twenty-year-old admirer was Jonathan Edwards—later to be the greatest theologian (and, some argue, the greatest philosopher

GET THE BIG

PICTURE

I. God Is Great
II. God Is Good
III. God Is Triune

and thinker) America has ever produced. The "young lady," who eventually became Edwards's wife, was Sarah Pierrepont. At the time Edwards penned this description of her, Sarah was *thirteen years old.*

This historical example demonstrates a point that is crucial to bear in mind as we embark on this study of theology proper, the study of God Himself. Theology is not just for older people. It is for all people, and the sooner a person begins the study, the better prepared that person will be to face life's challenges. For Sarah Pierrepont, a lifetime of theological learning and experience was required to carry her through the sudden loss of her husband. She was only

forty-eight, and many of the difficult responsibilities of life remained for her to bear alone. Nevertheless, at his death she wrote to one of her daughters, "A holy and good God has covered us with a dark cloud. O that we may kiss the rod, and lay our hands on our mouths! The Lord has done it. He has made me adore his goodness, that we had him [her husband] so long. But my God lives; and he has my heart. . . . We are

Jonathan Edwards (1703-1758) was a remarkably precocious youth. By the time he entered Yale at age thirteen, he knew Greek, Latin, and Hebrew and had written papers on philosophy. As Edwards grew older, it became evident that he was much more than an intellectual giant. His life was characterized by warm-hearted devotion to God. In 1724 he became pastor of the church in Northampton, Massachusetts. Under his leadership and preaching, the revival fires of the Great Awakening swept through his congregation in 1734-35. Later, Edwards was greatly used of the Lord to spread this revival to other parts of New England. His sermon "Sinners in the Hands of an Angry God," which he preached in 1741 in Enfield, Connecticut, remains one of the most famous sermons ever preached in the English language. Its passion, power, and spiritual impact make it unique as a compelling plea for the sinner's conversion.

all given to God; and there I am, and love to be." By knowing, believing, and cultivating the truths of Scripture, Sarah had come to the conviction that the triune God of the universe is both great and good. Have you?

God Is Great

Certainly none of us would seriously question that God is great. However, acknowledging that God is great and truly believing that He is great are two very different things. In fact, as A. W. Tozer noted some years ago, people who live fully aware of the greatness of God are uncommon indeed.

> The Church has surrendered her once lofty concept of God and has substituted for it one so low, so ignoble, as to be utterly unworthy of thinking, worshiping men. This she has done not deliberately, but little by little and without her knowledge; and her very unawareness only makes her situation all the more tragic. . . . This loss of the concept of majesty has come just when the forces of religion are making dramatic gains and the churches are more prosperous than at any time within the past several hundred years. But the alarming thing is that our gains are mostly external and our losses wholly internal. . . . If we would bring back spiritual power to our lives, we must begin to think of God more nearly as He is.

We may say that we believe God is great, but often our daily decisions contradict that claim. If we were truly convinced of God's greatness, a sincere sense of awe would characterize our public worship. We would be more afraid of sinning because we would be more fully aware that all our deeds are committed in the light of His presence. We also would be ashamed of stooping to use the world's means for accomplishing God's purposes in our churches and in our personal lives. Of course, by failing to reckon with the

reality of God's greatness, we do no damage to Him—He remains what He has always been. We do, however, cripple our spiritual effectiveness and our joy in the Lord. And, as Tozer noted, if we want to be spiritually whole, we must begin by thinking thoughts that are worthy of the only one who is able to make us whole.

God Is Spirit

The substance of God's being is entirely different from anything that we are able to imagine. He is not composed of matter and therefore does not have a body. Instead, as Christ told the Samaritan woman, "God is a Spirit" (John 4:24). Because His essence is spiritual and not material, God is free from the limitations of a body. He is not subject to decay and death (I Tim. 1:17), and the laws of physics that limit us to one location at a time do not apply to God. Paul explained to the Athenians that God's being is present with all of His creatures simultaneously: "In him we live, and move, and have our being" (Acts 17:27-28).

What Would You Say?

If God is spirit with no material, physical, tangible body parts, why does the Bible refer to the "hand" of God (Exod. 33:22), the "face" of God (Matt. 18:10), the "arm" of God (Exod. 15:16), or the "feet" of God (Nah. 1:3)?

Because God is a spirit, He is not visible to the human eye. In fact, His presence cannot be observed by any of the five senses. To reveal Himself to us, God moved on men to pen the Scripture, and He sent His Son into the world (John 1:18). Since our physical powers of observation cannot detect God, science is not an adequate means for knowing God or proving that He exists. For those who depend on science alone to define reality, God's invisibility makes Him irrelevant. But those who have a personal relationship with their Creator affirm—with Paul—that God's invisibility is a reason for praising Him (I Tim. 6:16).

God's spiritual being is also completely self-sufficient. Our fragile bodies depend on nourishment and a favorable environment to sustain them. God, however, depends on nothing outside Himself. God's self-sufficient nature should remind us that our service and worship do not meet some need that He has. God needs nothing. Serving God is a blessing that He allows us to enjoy. As Paul told the Athenians at Mars' Hill, "God . . . dwelleth not in temples made with hands; neither is worshipped with men's hands, as though he needed any thing, seeing he giveth to all life, and breath, and all things" (Acts 17:24-25). Such biblical statements put us in our proper place. We need God, but He does not need us.

Since God does not have a body, many religions (such as Hinduism) have supposed that He is an impersonal force. Scripture, however, clearly presents God as a person. Only a couple of pages into the Word of God, Scripture states that God communed with Adam and Eve (Gen. 3:8). A few chapters later, we are told that Enoch walked with God (Gen. 5:24). Later, Abraham is called the friend of God (James 2:23). And Moses is described as one who spoke with God "face to face, as a man speaketh unto his friend" (Exod. 33:11). God's willingness to engage His creatures in a personal relationship sets Him apart from the lost person's concept of

EXAMINE THE **CONTEXT**

The hallmark text for God's spirituality is John 4:24. Interestingly, this theological statement is situated within a very practical discussion regarding how God is to be worshiped. What does the context of this famous statement teach us about worshiping God?

deity. God offers us who trust in Him much more than eternal prosperity and happiness. He offers us Himself.

God Is Infinite

If God's spirituality mystifies us, then God's infinitude overwhelms us. Since we are finite beings, it is impossible for us to imagine any substance or person that is not limited in some way. God, however, knows no bounds. The following treatment will view God's infinity from three different angles. God is infinite in His relation to space, in His knowledge, and in His power.

Omnipresence

When we say that God is omnipresent, we mean that space places no limits on Him. Perhaps the best discussion of God's omnipresence is found in Psalm 139, where David extols God for His greatness: "Whither shall I go from thy spirit? or whither shall I flee from thy presence? If I ascend up into heaven, thou art there. . . . If I take the wings of the morning, and dwell in the uttermost parts of the sea; even there shall thy hand lead me, and thy right hand shall hold me" (vv. 7-10). We should note that omnipresence does not mean that God is infinitely large or that His substance fills the entire universe. God is independent of space; indeed, He created space. David states that anywhere he could go, God would be present there. Traveling to one part of the world does not bring a person to another part of God's being. God's entire being is present in every place.

The reality of God's omnipresence is a great comfort to the child of God. On the sunniest day, in the darkest midnight, in the most serene situation, in the vise of the most difficult trials—*God is there*. To enjoy the benefits of His presence, we need only to reach out to Him in faith by prayer. To the wicked, however,

What Would You Say?

Examine the following passages. What impact do they have on your understanding of God's omnipresence? How would you account for the details they present regarding God's presence?

—Exodus 33:1-4; I Samuel 4:19-22; Isaiah 55:6

God's omnipresence is a very fearful thing. Those who rebel against God's law do so always in the presence of the one who wrote that law and has promised to enforce it. For this reason the psalm that praises God for being omnipresent also observes, "Surely thou wilt slay the wicked, O God" (Ps. 139:19).

Omniscience

God is infinite in His knowledge as well. As the psalmist declares, "Great is our Lord, and of great power: his understanding is infinite" (Ps. 147:5). When we say that God is omniscient, we mean that He knows all things actual and possible. By *actual* we mean all that exists or has existed and all that has happened or is happening. The author of Hebrews clearly asserts God's infinite knowledge of His creation: "Neither is there any creature that is not manifest in his sight" (Heb. 4:13; see also Job 28:24). God's omniscience also extends to things possible. By *possible* we mean future things and events, as well as events that may happen but never do. In the book of Isaiah, God declares that because He understands the future perfectly, He alone is the true God. "I am God, and there is none like me, declaring the end from the beginning, and from ancient times the things that are not yet done" (Isa. 46:9-10). God also knows about events that never occur. When David was fleeing from Saul and asked the Lord whether the inhabitants of a certain city would betray him to the king, God replied, "They will deliver thee up" (I Sam. 23:12). With this information, David fled to another part of Israel and thus eluded King Saul.

We must remember that God's knowledge is not just extensive; it is also intensive. God knows each of us intimately—better than we know ourselves. In Psalm 139, David praises God for knowing everything about him: when he gets up in the morning, when he goes to bed, all the words that he speaks each day, and every thought that enters his mind. Later in the psalm, David exclaims, "How precious also are thy thoughts unto me, O God! how great is the sum of them! If I should count them, they are more in number than the sand" (Ps. 139:17-18). Anyone who seriously considers these words is compelled to echo David's conclusion regarding God's omniscience: "Such knowledge is too wonderful for me; it is high, I cannot attain unto it" (Ps. 139:6).

God is more than all-knowing, however. He is also all-wise (Rom. 11:33-34). We should never fear that we are known fully and intimately by a Being that will somehow misuse that knowledge. He always chooses the best goals, and He always employs the best means of reaching those goals. Realizing that God is all-wise should be a great encouragement to Christians, for He has assured believers that His goal for them is to make them eternally like His Son, Jesus

> *"God always chooses the best goals, and He always employs the best means of reaching those goals."*

Christ (Rom. 8:28-31). Truly, this goal is in our best interest. We must remember that His chosen means for reaching that goal is also in our best interest. Often it is difficult for us to believe that a family tragedy, the loss of a friendship, or the death of a loved one could somehow be part of God's plan for making us like His Son. We, however, hold in our hands only one piece of a gigantic puzzle. If we will live in the reality of this truth, we will at the end of our lives be able to affirm with David, "As for God, his way is perfect; . . . and he maketh my way perfect" (II Sam. 22:31, 33).

Omnipotence

It is not enough, however, for God to be omnipresent and omniscient. For God to triumph, He must also be able to implement what His wisdom directs Him to do. For this reason, the Bible constantly presents God as omnipotent. Scripture teaches that He is able to do whatever His perfect will has determined to do. Fifty-eight times the Bible refers to Him—and only Him—as "Almighty." This omnipotence is seen particularly in God's interaction with His people. When Sarah doubted that God was able to give her and Abraham a son, He rebuked her with the rhetorical question, "Is any thing too hard for the Lord?" (Gen. 18:14). When Christ told His disciples that it was easier for a camel to go through the eye of a needle than for a rich person to be saved, they replied, "Who then can be saved?" (Matt. 19:25). The Lord then reminded them, "With men this is impossible; but with God all things are possible" (v. 26). Consequently, God is completely free of external forces. Nothing outside of Him can compel Him to do anything. He also is free from all frustration. As the psalmist confidently asserted, "Our God is in the heavens: he hath done whatsoever he hath pleased" (Ps. 115:3).

It is not true, however, that God can do *anything*. He cannot do something that is contrary to His nature. God cannot lie (Heb. 6:18). He cannot even be tempted to do evil (James 1:13). For this reason we have defined omnipotence as God's being able to do whatever *His perfect will* has determined to do. Certainly, this qualification is no evidence of weakness in God's character. If it were possible for God to do something contrary to one of His other attributes, *that* would be a sign of tragic weakness.

God's omnipotence should fill us with awe, but it should also renew us spiritually. One of the reasons God has revealed to us that He is all-powerful is that He desires for us to enjoy the benefits of His infinite strength. For this reason many of the Bible's affirmations of God's omnipotence occur in passages designed to encourage God's people. Perhaps the best example of this encouragement is found in the book of Ephesians. When Paul concludes his prayer for the Ephesian believers, he assures them that God will answer his prayer, and he praises God for His omnipotence: "Now unto him that is able to do exceeding abundantly above all that we ask or think, according to the power that worketh in us, unto him be glory" (Eph. 3:20-21).

Read Deuteronomy 33:27 in context. This verse is a classic statement of God's eternality. Viewed in context, however, it is much more than simply a statement about God's relationship to time.

God Is Eternal

The Bible calls the Lord "the eternal God" because time does not apply to Him (Deut. 33:27). Moses praises the Lord for having no beginning: "Before the mountains were brought forth, or ever thou hadst formed the earth and the world, even from everlasting to everlasting, thou art God" (Ps. 90:2; see also Job 36:26). The Bible also indicates that God will never have an ending (Ps. 102:26-27).

Yet God's eternality involves more than just His having no beginning and no ending. He exists outside of time. Unlike human beings, He is not bound to viewing events in the three categories of past, present, and future. To us the present is near and vivid, the future is unknown, and the past exists in our minds in varying degrees of familiarity. Not so with God. He sees the past and the future with the same vividness and freshness with which He views the present. For this reason Peter is able to say, "One day is with the Lord as a thousand years, and a thousand years as one day" (II Pet. 3:8; see also Ps. 90:4). Many preachers have well illustrated this idea by comparing the passage of time to a train traveling through a valley. The person who stands in the valley can view the

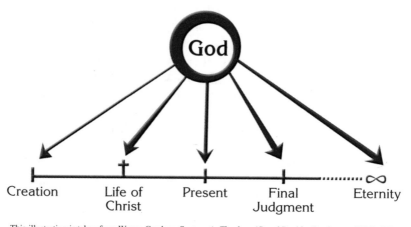

This illustration is taken from Wayne Grudem, *Systematic Theology* (Grand Rapids: Zondervan, 1994), 171.

train only one car at a time. However, the person who views the train from the top of a mountain sees all the cars simultaneously. Similarly, God stands outside of time and is able to view all of it at once.

God Is Unchanging

The Bible teaches that God is unchangeable in His attributes and in His purposes. Speaking specifically of His attributes of justice and patience, God affirms of Himself, "I am the Lord, I change not; therefore ye sons of Jacob are not consumed" (Mal. 3:6). Likewise, James assures his readers that God will always be the source of every good thing, for with Him "is no variableness, neither shadow of turning" (James 1:17). God is also unchanging in His purposes. His plan for the ages will never need to be amended: "The counsel of the Lord standeth for ever, the thoughts [lit., *plans*] of his heart to all generations" (Ps. 33:11).

We live in a world of disturbing change. Each of us could, without much effort, recite a litany of disappointments that we have suffered due to surprising changes in our friends—and perhaps even in our parents and church leaders. During such disappointments it is easy to think that the world is falling apart or spiraling out of control. But God does not change. He never has a bad day. He always acts and reacts in a way that is consistent with His character as it is revealed in Scripture. Even when we change and fail Him, He remains a solid rock on which we may rest and rely: "It is of the Lord's mercies that we are not consumed, because his compassions fail not" (Lam. 3:22).

God Is Good

From 1946 to 1952, J. B. Williams served as a missionary in West Africa. He quickly learned that his challenge was not to convince the Bariba tribesmen of God's existence. His labor was to correct the misconceptions of God that they and their traditions had formed.

The Baribas believe there is a supreme being, called "Gusunau" ("chief of the other side"), who has absolute authority and sovereignty over the universe. He also

11

possesses human characteristics, such as vengeance, wrath, and hate. To them, he isn't concerned about the welfare of man. . . .

There is fear in all phases of [a Bariba's life]. . . . When he sets out for his farm, with his short-handled hoe, he makes sure that he has amulets and charms on his body to protect him from evil spirits and disaster. In pursuing his way to the farm, he walks in a zigzag fashion because he believes that evil spirits go in a

When Williams and his family arrived in Benin, few Baribas knew the Lord.

straight line, and if he is walking in this fashion, evil spirits have less chance of overtaking him. Arriving at the farm, he makes sure he has a fire going so that the smoke ascending in the air will placate the evil spirits that may live around his farm.

The Baribas correctly perceived that they lived in a world of evil and that the power of evil was greater than their own. They also were able to discern that God was great. They failed, however, to realize that God is also *good.* He hates evil, and He loves man, whom He has made in His own image. Correcting the Baribas' beliefs concerning God proved to be not just a great challenge for Williams—it was also one of his most treasured joys.

By the time Williams left, hundreds had trusted Christ.

I was speaking in a village one day, and I was trying to convince them of the sinful nature of man and his

12

estranged condition from God. An old man spoke up saying, "That we know Batudi; we want to know what to do about it." I quoted John 3:16 in Bariba to him. . . . They had never heard that God loved them. I have seen old men, when they realized that God loved them and gave His Son for them at the cross, become so touched that tears would fill their eyes.

But one need not travel to Africa to observe misconceptions of God's character. Wherever the Scriptures are not taught and sincerely believed, dangerously incorrect thoughts about God abound. In the "Christianized" United States, unbelievers often refuse the gospel because they—like the Baribas—are suspicious that God does not have their best interests at heart. I have often heard unsaved people reject the gospel because they are convinced that such a decision would ruin their lives. Similarly, many Christian young people shrink from serving the Lord because they fear that He would call them to a life of tragedy and unhappiness. Do you believe that God is good? Do your daily choices reflect that belief? The following discussion is designed to convince our hearts of something that our minds have probably never doubted: *God is good.*

God Is Holy

When the prophet Isaiah was called to minister, the one divine attribute that overwhelmed him was God's holiness. The first words he heard in God's presence were the cries of the seraphim: "Holy, holy, holy, is the Lord of hosts" (Isa. 6:3). God revealed many wonderful truths about Himself to Isaiah during his long ministry, yet it is instructive to note that the first thing He revealed was His holiness. Without a proper appreciation for God's holiness, a person cannot understand any part of God's character as it is revealed in Scripture.

Uniqueness

As Isaiah 6 indicates, the Bible presents holiness in two different senses. In its most basic sense, God's holiness refers to the fact that He is separate from His creation. This majestic uniqueness is seen in the opening lines of Isaiah 6:1, "In the year that king

Uzziah died I saw also the Lord sitting upon a throne, high and lifted up." Other passages indicate that God's separateness above His creation is absolute and infinite. After crossing the Red Sea, Moses praises God: "Who is like unto thee, O Lord, among the gods? who is like thee, glorious in holiness, fearful in praises, doing wonders?" (Exod. 15:11). Perhaps the grandest passage arguing for God's uniqueness is Isaiah 40-46. Here the Lord comforts His people by telling them that He is infinitely exalted above their enemies, above their idols, and above them. At one point, after a gripping display of God's transcendence, the text concludes, "To whom then will ye liken me, or shall I be equal? saith the Holy One" (Isa. 40:25).

Because God is absolutely separate from everything else in the universe, He requires that His people treat Him as holy. While instructing the Israelites regarding proper worship, the Lord warned, "Neither shall ye profane [treat as ordinary] my holy name; but I will be hallowed [treated as holy] among the children of Israel" (Lev. 22:32). When God descended on Mount Sinai, He gave strict orders regarding the respect that His people were to show for His presence (Exod. 19:12). One of the tragedies of our day is that vast segments of Christianity do not evidence a proper view of God's holiness. This failure is particularly noticeable in public worship. We have emphasized the fact that God is personal to the point that we are losing sight of His holiness. God is not "one of us." He is personal and He does engage His creatures in personal relationships, but He is a person infinitely beyond us in majesty and glory. Therefore, we must be careful to avoid music or speech that degrades His majesty or treats Him as a fellow creature.

Purity

If uniqueness were the only idea communicated by the word *holiness,* then this attribute would belong in our discussion of

The following quotation makes a theological statement about the character of God. Would you consider it truth or error? "Through a continual course of progression, our heavenly Father has received exaltation and glory, and he points us out the same path; and inasmuch as he is clothed with power, authority, and glory, he says, 'walk ye up and come in possession of the same glory and happiness that I possess.'"

In response to Isaiah's confession, God sent a seraph to purge the prophet's lips with a coal from His altar (Isa. 6:6-7).

God's greatness. There is, however, a moral application of God's holiness. When we say that God is holy, we not only mean that He is unique; we also mean that He is absolutely pure. This matchless purity stung the conscience of Isaiah when he beheld the Holy One of Israel in His temple: "Woe is me! for I am undone; because I am a man of unclean lips, and I dwell in the midst of a people of unclean lips" (Isa. 6:5). The prophet Habakkuk recognized this aspect of God's holiness when he prayed, "Thou art of purer eyes than to behold evil, and canst not look on iniquity" (Hab. 1:13). The apostle John demonstrated that God's holiness is fundamental to a correct understanding of deity when he wrote, "This then is the message which we have heard of him, and declare unto you, that God is light, and in him is no darkness at all" (I John 1:5).

Recognizing this aspect of God's holiness is one of the most practical considerations in theological study. The Bible teaches that those who claim to be God's children are to imitate Him in His holiness. As He Himself has said, "Be ye holy; for I am holy" (I Pet. 1:16). Believers must lead pure lives that will set them apart from this sinful world. Some of the most common applications of holiness in the Word of God concern abstaining from lust and loving others sincerely (I Pet. 1:13-22).

God Is True

When we say that God is true, we mean that He is completely reliable, and throughout Scripture this reliability is affirmed primarily in three ways. First of all, *God is reliable in His person—* He is who He claims to be. Frequently in the Old Testament, God contrasts Himself with the gods of the other nations. Whereas their claims to deity are false, His are entirely true (Jer. 10:9-10). Second, *God is reliable in the way that He represents reality.* He cannot lie. All of His communications with man are true (Titus 1:2; see also Prov. 30:5-6; John 17:17). Third, *God is reliable in the way that He interacts with His creatures.* By this statement we mean that God is faithful. He does what He says He will do. He keeps all His promises. When Balak, king of Moab, tried to convince Balaam to curse the Israelites, Balaam explained that God's truthfulness would not permit him to curse those whom He had promised to bless: "God is not a man, that he should lie; neither the son of man, that he should repent: hath he said, and shall he not do it? or hath he spoken, and shall he not make it good?" (Num. 23:19).

God's truthfulness places a significant burden on mankind. Because God always tells the truth, He expects His creatures to be truthful as well. He hates lying (Prov. 6:16-17), and He has promised that no one who lives in deception will escape eternal punishment: "All liars, shall have their part in the lake which burneth with fire and brimstone: which is the second death" (Rev. 21:8). God also expects His creatures to act faithfully. We are to be faithful in our relationships with others (Josh. 9:16-19; Mal. 2:13-16), and God expects us to be faithful to Him (Eccles. 5:4-5). Such expectations may seem daunting, but, as Paul affirms, we can be confident that God will faithfully help those who trust Him: "The very God of peace sanctify you wholly. . . . Faithful is he that calleth you, who also will do it" (I Thess. 5:23-24).

"'Inspiration' means 'filling with Spirit.' It is not only a religious term but also an artistic one. A great piece of music or literature or painting may be recognized as 'inspired,' by which we mean that it appears to express something of more than human origin. . . . The Christian claim about the Scriptures is that in them we hear the Word of God. That means that, like all inspired works, the Bible gives a true account of the world. It need not be scientifically true, in detail, nor even historically accurate; but it must be true in the larger sense that it calls to our attention those things which are most significant in our universe and places them in a right perspective. The Bible differs from other inspired works, not in that it is 'more' inspired, but in that its inspiration, stemming from the Creator himself, gives a fuller and truer perspective than that of any other work."

In Genesis 18:25 Abraham claims God's righteous character as the basis for his plea that Lot and his family be delivered from Sodom. God was moved by this request, even though Lot and his family were imperiled in Sodom because of their own unrighteous choices. How is it that God's righteousness was the basis for Abraham's plea for His mercy on Lot?

God Is Righteous

"Righteous art thou, O Lord, and upright are thy judgments" (Ps. 119:137). One of the first things that God teaches those who follow Him is that He is righteous. Abraham was so convinced that God was righteous that he could stand in His presence and boldly ask the rhetorical question, "Shall not the Judge of all the earth do right?" (Gen. 18:25).

A person is considered righteous if he conforms to a given standard. Consequently whenever the word *right* or *righteous* is used, the presence of a standard, or a code of conduct, is assumed. In Scripture God is the perfect standard, and His law expresses the ramifications of His moral perfections for human behavior. Because God is perfect, His law is also perfect (Ps. 19:7). Therefore, God is righteous in a sense that no man—not even a perfect man—could ever hope to be. For human beings, the law of God is an external standard that stands over them, telling them how to live. No law is above God, however. Nevertheless, God cannot commit acts that violate His law because His law is the expression of His character. Therefore, when we say that God is righteous, we mean that His character (expressed in His law) defines what is right and that His acts are always in agreement with His character.

To have a proper appreciation for the righteousness of God, we also must give some consideration to His law, and although a detailed treatment would be out of place here, we should devote some space to the law's most important requirement. When Christ was asked which command in the law was the greatest, He responded without hesitation, "Thou shalt love the Lord thy God with all thy heart" (Mark 12:30). The fundamental moral obligation for everyone in the universe—including God—is to love God completely. At this point it becomes apparent that we cannot get an accurate view of God by assuming that He is like us, just infinitely wiser and more powerful. God is divine, and we are human.

Think About It!

Many people find God's passion for His own glory to be offensive. Often they base this disapproval on their observation of other humans. Men and women who love themselves supremely are selfish and unpleasant to live with. But consider the life and ministry of Jesus Christ. The Lord came to earth to explain by His deeds the character of God the Father (John 1:18). At one point He declared, "He that hath seen me hath seen the Father" (John 14:9). Yet as God's representative, He was never selfish. He openly taught that He did not come to be served but to serve and die for others (Mark 10:45). He worked countless miracles, and none of them harmed anyone. Every miracle was designed to relieve human suffering. Nevertheless, men hated Him and plotted His death. Amazingly, as He was dying, He loved even His executors and prayed, "Father, forgive them; for they know not what they do" (Luke 23:34). Truly, no one ever loved as Jesus loved.

He is fundamentally different from us. Because we are finite, created beings, it would be wrong for us to love ourselves first and foremost. God, however, is the infinite, most valuable, and most glorious being in the universe. It is only right for Him to love Himself supremely. If He were to love something else supremely, He would be committing idolatry. We should not be alarmed, therefore, that God's greatest concern is to glorify Himself (Ezek. 36:22-23; John 14:13; Rom. 11:36; Eph. 3:9-11). We also should not be offended by the fact that God is a jealous God (Exod. 20:5; 34:14). He not only has a right to demand that every being in the universe love Him completely, but He also is right to demand that love—to do anything else would be unrighteous.

God Is Just

"He is the Rock, his work is perfect: for all his ways are judgment: a God of truth and without iniquity, just and right is he" (Deut. 32:4). As this verse indicates, God's righteousness and justice are closely related to each other. Righteousness refers to the fact that God perfectly conforms to His own standard. Justice means that He holds all other beings accountable to live by that same standard. Theologians often divide God's justice into two categories. *Remunerative justice* refers to God's rewarding those who do good with blessings. *Retributive justice* refers to God's punishing those who do evil. Perhaps the most succinct expression

"Many deny the strict punitive justice of God and claim that God punishes the sinner to reform him, or to deter others from sin; but these positions are not tenable. The primary purpose of the punishment of sin is the maintenance of right and justice. Of course, it may incidentally serve, and may even, secondarily, be intended, to reform the sinner and to deter others from sin."

of both of these aspects is found in Paul's letter to the Romans: "[God] will render to every man according to his deeds: to them who by patient continuance in well doing seek for glory and honour and immortality, eternal life: but unto them that are contentious, and do not obey the truth, but obey unrighteousness, indignation and wrath" (Rom. 2:6-8).

Repeatedly in Scripture God reminds His people that He is completely impartial in the execution of His justice (II Chron. 19:7; Eph. 6:9). He does not favor the rich over the poor, the powerful over the weak. This total lack of favoritism is perhaps best seen in His use of death. Long ago in the Garden of Eden, the Lord warned Adam and Eve that if they sinned, they would die. Since then all

What Would You Say?

Read Matthew 20:1-16. What impact do these verses have on your understanding of God's justice? Does God appear fair to you in this passage?

sinners in each generation, regardless of their attainments, suffer death. As finite beings who live on earth for only a few decades, we often have difficulty believing that God is indeed completely just. Many of God's people throughout history have endured difficult circumstances that have led them to question God's justice (e.g., Ps. 73:2-14). Faith and time, however, will convince the devout heart that God's words to Moses long ago are inviolable: "The Lord, The Lord God . . . [He] will by no means clear the guilty" (Exod. 34:6-7).

God Is Loving

The portrait that we are attempting to paint of God's character would be far from complete—and quite misleading—if we stopped here. God is more than righteous, just, true, and holy. We must never forget the apostle John's comforting reminder, "God is love" (I John 4:8). Woven into the fabric of God's infinite nature is an incomprehensible capacity to love others. Tragically, many people misunderstand God's love because they do not understand what biblical love is. If we are to know what "God is love" means, we must endeavor to understand the biblical definition of love.

The apostle Paul gives an amazingly succinct definition of love in I Corinthians 13. Here he captures the essence of love by naming its two essential manifestations: "Charity [love] suffereth long, and is kind" (v. 4). This statement describes love negatively and positively. According to Paul, a person shows his love by being patient—not doing certain negative deeds that the object of his love may deserve. A person also shows love by being kind, that is, doing kind deeds in order to benefit the person loved.

Kindness

The kindness of God may be viewed from several different angles. From the most general perspective, God's kindness is His **benevolence.** This word describes God's concern to accomplish the good of those He loves. God demonstrated His benevolence in the Garden of Eden when He observed, "It is not good that the man should be alone; I will make him an help meet for him" (Gen. 2:18). Although Adam was unaware that he was incomplete, God knew, and He provided for Adam's need. Adam is certainly not the only recipient of God's benevolence. Every day God shows His kind concern for the welfare of plants and animals. The psalmist revealed this fact when he prayed, "Thou openest thine hand, and satisfiest the desire of every living thing" (Ps. 145:16). The apostle Paul, speaking to the inhabitants of Lystra, argued for God's existence by asserting His benevolence for all people:

EXAMINE THE CONTEXT

"God is love"—those three words from I John 4:8 communicate one of the best known sentences in all of Scripture. The verses that surround the statement are not very well known, however. Interestingly, they do not concern the character of God alone. They also have a great deal to say about believers. According to that passage, why is it important for believers to understand that God is love?

BENEVOLENCE

"[God] left not himself without witness, in that he did good, and gave us rain from heaven, and fruitful seasons, filling our hearts with food and gladness" (Acts 14:17). And Christ taught that even the wicked are recipients of God's kind care, for God "maketh his sun to rise on the evil and on the good, and sendeth rain on the just and on the unjust" (Matt. 5:45). But the highest degree of God's benevolence is reserved for His followers. His concern for the welfare of believers elevates them to a remarkably exalted status. The night He was betrayed, the Lord revealed, "These things have I spoken unto you, that my joy might remain in you, and that your joy might be full. . . . Greater love hath no man than this, that a man lay down his life for his friends. Ye are my friends" (John 15:11, 13-14).

More specifically, God shows His kindness through His **mercy.** The word *mercy* refers to God's stooping to help those who are in a pitiful condition. As fallen, sinful human beings, we tend to be repulsed by the pitiful condition of another—particularly if he has caused his condition. Such a lowly, shameful state does not repulse God. Rather, it moves Him to show compassion. David found encouragement in telling God that He was "plenteous in mercy unto all them that call upon thee" (Ps. 86:5). By the end of his life, David had learned to depend on God's mercy. After foolishly numbering the people in his kingdom, David was confronted by the prophet Gad, who told him that he could be punished through his enemies or through the direct working of God. Broken, David responded, "Let us fall into the hand of the Lord; for his mercies are great" (II Sam. 24:14). Mercy was a hallmark of Jesus' ministry. Even when a man with leprosy asked for a healing touch, Jesus was not repulsed or bothered (Mark 1:41). The mercy of our Lord was also seen in His concern for the spiritual needs of people. The sight of a large crowd did not annoy or weary Him: "When he saw the multitudes, he was moved with compassion on

MERCY

them, because they fainted, and were scattered abroad, as sheep having no shepherd" (Matt. 9:36).

Finally, God demonstrates His kindness through His **grace.** Again, we should note God's words to Moses at Sinai: "The Lord, The Lord God, merciful and gracious" (Exod. 34:6). In the Bible the grace of God refers to His showing favor to those who deserve punishment. If mercy is having compassion on a helpless beggar, then grace is showing favor to a convicted criminal.

God takes great delight in demonstrating this aspect of His love. Grace is the basis of the salvation that He offers to man in His Son, Jesus Christ. As we reflect on our many sins, we may be tempted to think that God wants us to reform our lives so that we may deserve His favor. We, however, can never deserve God's favor. The right response to God's goodness is not a steely resolve to be good. God simply asks for humble faith: "[Salvation] is of faith, that it might be by grace" (Rom. 4:16). Those who try to work their way into finding God's favor only frustrate His purpose in saving sinners, for God has so ordered salvation that everyone who is delivered from sin must glorify Him for His amazing grace. By delivering people from sin through His grace alone, He declares Himself to be the incomparably great and good God: "That in the ages to come he might shew the exceeding riches of his grace in his kindness toward us through Christ Jesus. For by grace are ye saved through faith; and that not of yourselves: it is the gift of God: not of works, lest any man should boast" (Eph. 2:7-9).

Grace does not end with the conversion of the sinner, however. The reality of God's unmerited favor is to be the saint's constant source of strength and encouragement. Paul told Timothy not to face the struggles of the Christian life in his own strength but to find strength "in the grace that is in Christ Jesus" (II Tim. 2:1). Peter closed his second epistle exhorting his readers to "grow in grace, and in the knowledge of our Lord and Saviour Jesus Christ" (II Pet. 3:18). But how do we come to enjoy this enabling favor for our spiritual growth? We follow the example of the Apostle Paul. He began and ended nearly every one of his epistles with the indirect prayer, "Grace be with you" (e.g., Col. 4:18). If the right way to get grace for others is to pray, then surely the right way to get grace for ourselves is to pray for it ourselves. As we pray daily for this grace, we should remember Christ's promise, "If ye shall ask any thing in my name, I will do it" (John 14:14). Do not doubt that God will answer your prayers— remember, *He loves you.*

Patience

Because God loves, God is patient. When the Lord declared His goodness to Moses on Mount Sinai, He was careful to include among His descriptions of Himself the adjective "longsuffering" (Exod. 34:6). This word, not common in our language anymore, paints a beautiful picture of one manifestation of divine love. God suffers with the rebellion of sinful people for a long time. He delights in holding back the fury of His just anger. Peter explains that God's patience was the reason that it took Noah 120 years to build the ark (I Pet. 3:20; Gen. 6:3). It was the longsuffering of God that necessitated the Israelite sojourn in Egypt. The Lord refused to give Canaan to Abraham and his immediate descendants because "the iniquity of the Amorites is not yet full" (Gen. 15:16). And Peter reveals that the reason Jesus Christ has not yet returned is that God is longsuffering, "not willing that any should perish" (II Pet. 3:9). We should not think that this remarkable patience reveals some weakness in God's character, as though He lacks the courage to execute justice. God has a definite purpose in withholding His just anger. Paul reveals that God suffers long with sinners to encourage them to repent (Rom. 2:4).

As believers whose spirits wince at the sight of injustice and wickedness, we are often tempted to doubt the righteousness of God. "Why does God wait so long to right the wrongs in this world?" we often wonder. The apostles James and John had a similar feeling when a village in Samaria refused to receive Jesus and His followers. "Lord, wilt thou that we command fire to come down from heaven, and consume them?" they asked Christ. But Jesus rebuked them, "Ye know not what manner of spirit ye are of. For the Son of man is not come to destroy men's lives, but to save them" (Luke 9:54-56). The Bible later reveals that the

Spirit of God did a great work in that same area after Christ's ascension (Acts 8). We are all debtors to God's longsuffering love. Although we can never pay that debt, we can demonstrate that we recognize our debt by rejoicing in God's patience rather than despising it.

God Is Triune

It was something like walking through a buzz saw. There we were—my friend and I—trying to argue with a Jehovah's Witness about the deity of Christ. We did not get very far in our presentation of the biblical evidence before we were interrupted. "Listen, I've been an elder with the Jehovah's Witnesses since 1971, and none of you guys has ever been able to answer this question. Tell me. Does the word *Trinity* ever occur in the Bible?" I thought for a moment. "To my knowledge, no—it never does." Then he fired back, "Why do you teach something that's not in the Bible? You know, God doesn't like it when people add to His Word!" Our conversation deteriorated rather quickly after that.

In considering the doctrine of the Trinity, we learn that systematic theology is vitally important to understanding God's revelation. As we mentioned earlier, systematic theology collects information regarding certain themes found throughout the Bible and summarizes them in a coherent fashion. When it comes to the Trinity, we cannot point to a single verse to prove the doctrine—as we can with each of the preceding attributes of God. Nevertheless, the fact that God is triune is taught throughout the Bible. The only way to discern this teaching, however, is by using systematic theology. By collecting and organizing the Bible's statements regarding the Father, the Son, and the Holy Spirit, we learn that believing in the Trinity is not adding to God's Word. Indeed, rejecting the Trinity would be heresy—it would amount to subtracting from God's Word.

GET THE BIG PICTURE

Describing the Trinity

I. There Is One God

II. Three Persons Are Identified as God

III. These Three Persons Are Distinct

EXAMINE THE CONTEXT Another important passage concerning the deity of Christ is John 12:37-41. John's use of Isaiah's prophecy provides an important window into the Bible's understanding of Jesus' identity.

There Is One God

From the beginning of His revelation, God presents Himself as one being and as the only one of His kind. For this reason, the Israelites were not allowed to worship other gods: "I am the first, and I am the last; and beside me there is no God" (Isa. 44:6; see also 44:8; 45:5). The New Testament writers echo this teaching. James and Paul both teach in clear language that there is only one God (James 2:19; I Tim. 2:5-6). Sometimes people ask what pagans are doing when they worship a god other than the God of the Bible. Paul explains that such worship is not offered to a deity; it is offered to demons (I Cor. 8:4-6; 10:20).

Three Persons Are Identified as God

The Father Is God

No one familiar with biblical teaching would question that the Father is God. Jesus clearly taught the deity of the Father, referring to Him as "God the Father" (John 6:27). Paul also taught that the Father is God: "There is but one God, the Father, of whom are all things, and we in him" (I Cor. 8:6).

The Son Is God

Through the centuries many have questioned the deity of Jesus Christ. Scripture, however, clearly teaches that Jesus is not only the Son of God but is also God the Son. In the first lines of John's Gospel, He is called God: "In the beginning was the Word, and the Word was with God, and the Word was God" (John 1:1). After His resurrection Christ appeared to the disciples, and when Thomas saw Him, he said to Jesus, "My Lord and my God" (John 20:28).

In Scripture Jesus is not only called God, but He is also treated as God. On several occasions during His earthly ministry, people bowed down and worshiped Him (Matt. 8:2; Mark 5:6; Luke 24:52; John 9:38). This is an important observation because created beings are not allowed to accept worship. Such devotion is recognized to be worthy of God alone (Acts 12:21-23; 14:13-15; Rev. 19:10). Christ, however, never refused the worship of others. On one occasion, in fact, He demanded it (John 5:21-23). And in eternity Jesus Christ's claim to worship will be vindicated, for one day all will bow their knees and worship Him (Phil. 2:9-10; see also Rev. 5:8-14).

Scripture also demonstrates Christ's deity by ascribing to Him works that are unique to deity. Jesus Christ created the world (John 1:3). He currently sustains the entire universe by His own power (Col. 1:17; Heb. 1:3). He is able to forgive sins (Luke 5:20-21). He will one day resurrect the dead (John 5:25). And in the day of judgment, Jesus Christ Himself will be the Judge (John 5:22).

The Holy Spirit Is God

The Bible teaches that the Holy Spirit is divine as well. In several places *God* and *Holy Spirit* are used interchangeably

THEOLOGY & HISTORY

The year was A.D. 325, and Emperor Constantine (who had been converted about ten years earlier) invited several hundred leaders of the Christian church to the city of Nicea. The churches of the Roman Empire were divided over the question of Christ's identity. Several years earlier Arius of Alexandria, a popular preacher, had attacked his bishop for teaching that the relationship between Christ and the Father was a mystery. Charging that believing in the Trinity denied the distinctions that exist between the Father and the Son, Arius preached that Christ was not God but a created being. At the Council of Nicea, Arius clashed with Athanasius, a head deacon from Alexandria. Athanasius, little more than thirty years old, countered that Jesus Christ was eternal, uncreated, and of the same essence as the Father. Unless this were so, he argued, Christ could not have purchased salvation for mankind. Athanasius succeeded in making his case. The council formulated a creed based, in part, on his statements. Although the council condemned Arianism, denial of Christ's deity persisted—as it does to this day. Presently, the most common proponents of the Arian heresy are the Jehovah's Witnesses.

(John 14:16-17, 23; Acts 5:3-4; I Cor. 3:16-17). Scripture also indicates that He enjoys a status equal to the Father and the Son. The apostles were told to baptize in "the name of the Father, and of the Son, and of the Holy Ghost" (Matt. 28:19). The Spirit is similarly exalted in other contexts (II Cor. 13:14; I Pet. 1:2). On one occasion Jesus stated that the Spirit was to receive even more honor than He. Although blasphemy against the Son of God could be forgiven, blasphemy against the Holy Spirit was, according to Christ, unpardonable (Matt. 12:31-32). The Bible also teaches that the Holy Spirit does the works of God. He was involved in creating the world (Gen. 1:2; Job 26:13). He regenerates sinners to new life in Christ (John 3:8). He convicts unrighteous people of their sin and guides believers in their Christian walk (John 16:8; Rom. 8:14). Furthermore, the Bible teaches that the Spirit possesses divine attributes. He has infinite understanding, for He understands the mind of God (I Cor. 2:11-16). He also is eternal in His nature (Heb. 9:14).

These Three Persons Are Distinct

Since three persons are identified as God in Scripture, and since there is only one God, many believers have concluded that the distinctions between the Father, the Son, and the Holy Spirit are superficial. Evidently, these names refer to the different functions that God plays in His interaction with man. Sometimes He reveals Himself as an almighty father, sometimes as a spirit, and sometimes as a man. However, careful study of the biblical evidence demonstrates that this conclusion misrepresents the Scripture's teaching.

The baptismal formula that Christ commanded His followers to use indicates that the Father, Son, and Holy Spirit are in fact three distinct persons (Matt. 28:19). Furthermore, in Christ's

"We believe in one God, the Father Almighty . . . and in one Lord Jesus Christ, the only begotten Son of God, begotten of the Father before all worlds, Light of Light, very God of very God, begotten, not made, being of one substance with the Father . . . and in the Holy Ghost, who is Lord and Giver of life, who proceedeth from the Father, who with the Father and the Son together is worshipped and glorified."

teaching He regularly referred to the Father and the Holy Spirit in the third person, implying that the three were not the same person. Christ also frequently prayed to the Father—an activity that would be bizarre, at best, if the two were in fact the same person.

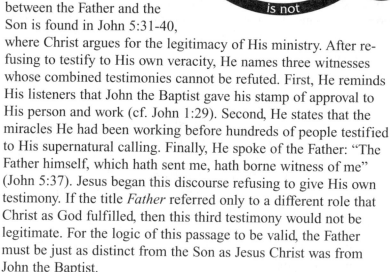

Perhaps the best proof of the distinction between the Father and the Son is found in John 5:31-40, where Christ argues for the legitimacy of His ministry. After refusing to testify to His own veracity, He names three witnesses whose combined testimonies cannot be refuted. First, He reminds His listeners that John the Baptist gave his stamp of approval to His person and work (cf. John 1:29). Second, He states that the miracles He had been working before hundreds of people testified to His supernatural calling. Finally, He spoke of the Father: "The Father himself, which hath sent me, hath borne witness of me" (John 5:37). Jesus began this discourse refusing to give His own testimony. If the title *Father* referred only to a different role that Christ as God fulfilled, then this third testimony would not be legitimate. For the logic of this passage to be valid, the Father must be just as distinct from the Son as Jesus Christ was from John the Baptist.

In every generation of the Christian church, scholars have attempted to find some analogy or explanation that would enable people to understand the Trinity. Such scholars must keep returning to the wise advice of John Calvin. Concerning the relationship between the members of the Trinity, he once commented, "It is far safer to rest contented with the relation as taught by [God] than get bewildered in vain speculation by subtle prying into a sublime mystery." In another place, speaking of those who have propounded heresy while trying to explain the doctrine,

Calvin warns that we ought "never to attempt to search after God anywhere but in his sacred word, and never to speak or think of him farther than we have it for our guide." God did inspire the Scripture in order to make Himself known to man, but we must never forget that God is ultimately incomprehensible. His being and character are so great that we can never understand Him fully, and accepting that He is ultimately unknowable is essential to knowing Him truly.

Conclusion

What is God? "God is a Spirit, infinite, eternal, and unchangeable, in his being, wisdom, power, holiness, justice, goodness, and truth"—so reads the fourth question and answer in the Westminster *Shorter Catechism.* To those who do not know God but are familiar with the study of theology, the answer is an amazingly brief yet comprehensive summary of the attributes of God. For those who know God and theology, however, the answer is much more. It is a reminder of the marvelous privilege that belongs to believers, for as the Westminster theologians imply in their first question, this great, good, and mysteriously triune God desires to share the excellencies of His marvelous being with His creatures. *What is the chief end of man?* "Man's chief end is to glorify God, and to enjoy him for ever." If we are believers, this God is our God. We are in Him, and He in us.

In the midst of civil war, the English Parliament commissioned the Westminster Assembly. This group of 151 Puritans gathered in Westminster Abbey from 1643-1649 to advise Parliament in establishing a church in England that seemed to them to agree most with Scripture. One responsibility of these theologians was to formulate a detailed creed of the Christian faith. The resulting Westminster *Confession of Faith* has become the classic expression of Christian doctrine for most Presbyterian churches and many Baptist groups. The Assembly's most influential work, *The Shorter Catechism,* is a series of 107 questions and answers. Originally intended as a doctrinal guide for children, the catechism has trained millions of believers, young and old, in the fundamental doctrines of Christianity.

Westminster Abbey

Holy, Holy, Holy

Reginald Heber, 1783-1826

Holy, Holy, Holy! Lord God Almighty!
Early in the morning our song shall rise to Thee;
Holy, Holy, Holy! Merciful and Mighty!
God in Three Persons, blessed Trinity!

Holy, Holy, Holy! All the saints adore Thee,
Casting down their golden crowns around the glassy sea;
Cherubim and seraphim falling down before Thee,
Which wert and art, and evermore shalt be.

Holy, Holy, Holy! Tho' the darkness hide Thee,
Tho' the eye of sinful man Thy glory may not see,
Only Thou art holy; there is none beside Thee
Perfect in power, in love, and purity.

Holy, Holy, Holy! Lord God Almighty!
All Thy works shall praise Thy name, in earth, and sky, and sea;
Holy, Holy, Holy! Merciful and Mighty!
God in Three Persons, blessed Trinity!

CHAPTER TWO

His Mighty Acts

2

Memory Verses: Psalm 33:8-11

History, art, architecture, literature, philosophy, and a host of boldly adventurous deities—culturally the Greeks of the first century had it all. Certainly Paul faced a daunting task when he entered the world of the Greeks with the gospel. His religion was

based on the testimony of a Jesus from Nazareth who was rejected even by His own people. He died in humiliation on a Roman cross, and although Paul believed He had been raised from the dead, none of the Greeks in Greece or Asia Minor had seen Him. How could Paul expect any

of these people to forsake Zeus and the rest of the pantheon for his Jesus? *But forsake them they did.* In Philippi, Thessalonica, Berea, Athens, and Corinth, converts came to Christ and publicly professed their allegiance to the Father, the Son, and the Holy Spirit. The Greek world would never be the same. The day that Paul began preaching the gospel in Greece was the day that faith in Zeus began to die. Today people do still commonly observe, "All men are Greeks." And while this statement does to a degree reflect continued Greek influence on education, architecture, and language, it does not reflect Greek influence on religion. Belief in Zeus is a relic of the past; belief in Jesus continues to change the world.

GET THE BIG

PICTURE

I. Creation
   A. Biblical Evidence
   B. Implications of the Evidence
II. Providence
   A. Preservation
   B. Government
   C. Miracles

The Greeks worshiped many gods, but Zeus was their chief deity. As the supreme ruler, he was to uphold law, justice, and morality. Nevertheless, Zeus was often involved in immoral liaisons with goddesses who captured his fancy. This weakness frequently got him into trouble. On one occasion Gaia, the goddess of the earth, warned Zeus that the unborn child from a recent escapade with Metis (the goddess of prudence, ironically) could eventually overthrow him. To protect his authority, Zeus swallowed Metis. Outraged, Hephaestus, one of Zeus's children and the god of fire, attacked Zeus and split open his head. From this wound emerged the daughter that Metis had been bearing—Athena, the goddess of wisdom, art, and warfare. Being a god, Zeus quickly recovered from his head trauma, though he probably never completely overcame the blow to his reputation.

When one considers the important differences between the ancient Greek concept of deity and the God of the Bible, the gospel's conquest in that part of the world is no mystery. Despite their learning and their many accomplishments, the Greeks knew nothing of a god whose acts proved he was infinitely great and infinitely good. The acts of their deities exposed them as finite, morally depraved, and incapable of governing the world effectively. Paul, however, preached about a God whose mighty deeds demonstrated that He deserved mankind's total devotion. In a sermon to the Athenians at Mars' Hill, Paul declared that his God alone created the universe (Acts 17:24, 26), that He providentially preserves His creatures (vv. 25-26), and that He governs the world according to His own plan (vv. 26-27, 31). Paul did not present these works of God as abstract concepts. In his conclusion he warned that since all of them were part of God's world, they were accountable to Him. Paul urged them, therefore, to repent of their sins because his God "hath appointed a day, in the which he will judge the world in righteousness" (vv. 30-31). As happened throughout the Greek world, when Paul finished preaching, some of those listening embraced his teaching and believed (v. 34).

The same works of God that Paul declared in ancient Greece are the subject of this chapter. And the same application that the apostle drew from those works will give significance to our study. Since God made the world and governs it, we are accountable to Him. Each of us is either with Him or against Him in His working. If we oppose Him, we, with Zeus and all his devotees, will certainly be defeated. If, however, we are on His side we will be victorious, and we will know the joy of being part of that king-dom whose citizens forever obey the happy command: "Praise him for his mighty acts" (Ps. 150:2).

God's Work of Creation

The importance of understanding God's work of creation is demonstrated by its placement in Scripture. The first sentence in the Bible asserts, "In the beginning God created the heaven and the earth" (Gen. 1:1). For more than two centuries, much of the

scientific community has opposed the idea that the universe was created by a direct act of God. Scientists have claimed that the world came into being through a long period of evolution, or development. Supposedly, this development took place over billions of years and is generally explained as the work of natural processes, not the work of an omnipo-tent God. In the wake of this attack, many believers have left Christianity's traditional

teaching about creation and opted for one closer to science's idea of evolution. It is certainly important, therefore, for us to know what exactly the Bible says about God's creative work and what implications we should derive from the Bible's teaching.

Biblical Evidence

Ex Nihilo

More and more, people who view themselves as Christians are embracing the ancient beliefs of pantheism and dualism. *Pantheism* teaches that the universe is an emanation of the divine essence. Therefore, everything in the universe is somehow part of the

Sometimes the history of science intersects the history of theology. Such was the case with the development of the theory of evolution, particularly Darwinian evolution. Once the effects of Charles Darwin's *Origin of Species* (published in 1859) were felt, those who believed that the universe was created by the direct act of God were considered unlearned. The following sentence from the end of Darwin's introduction tolled the end of widespread belief in the Bible's account of man's origin—for scientists as well as theologians and preachers.

"Although much remains obscure, and will long remain obscure, I can entertain no doubt, after the most deliberate study and dispassionate judgment of which I am capable, that the view which most naturalists until recently entertained, and which I formerly entertained—namely, that each species has been independently created—is erroneous."

Supreme Being. Pantheistic religions usually encourage their followers to engage in meditation that is supposed to help them realize their place in the universe and blend into the divine essence. This worldview is essential to a number of Eastern religions, such as Taoism, Buddhism, and Hinduism. It is also surprisingly common among some of the more educated people in the West. *Dualism,* on the other hand, teaches that there are two eternal forces in the universe. Many dualistic religions identify these forces as God and matter, and they believe that the conflict between good and evil is eternal. Many of those in the New Age Movement are dualistic in their worldview.

(Pantheism)

(Dualism)

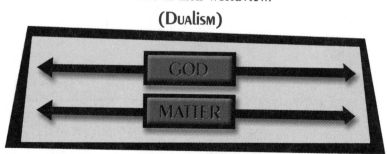

The doctrine of creation *ex nihilo* directly contradicts both of these worldviews. When we say that God created the world *ex nihilo* (Latin, "out of nothing"), we mean that He used no preexisting materials. Scripture teaches that everything in the universe—other than God—is temporal and created. Genesis 1:1 says that in the beginning the entire universe ("the heaven and the earth") came into existence by God's creative work. Speaking of Christ, John states, "All things were made by him; and without him was not anything made that was made" (John 1:3). Paul explains that "all things" applies not just to the material world: "By [Christ] were all things created, that are in heaven, and that are in earth, visible and invisible" (Col. 1:16).

Despite these verses one could still deny that the Bible teaches creation *ex nihilo* by supposing that God created the world from His own substance. The first chapter of Genesis, however, rejects this idea. It gives no indication that the divine essence was somehow used as the universe's building blocks. Rather it states that God spoke the world into existence, creation by *fiat* (Latin, "let it be"). In His creative work, the Lord simply ordered, "Let there be" (Gen. 1:3-26). In none of these pronouncements does God indicate that the beings and substances resulting would somehow be an emanation of His spiritual substance. Other Bible passages emphasize the doctrine of creation by *fiat*. The psalmist declares, "By the word of the Lord were the heavens made; . . . For he spake, and it was done; he commanded, and it stood fast" (Ps. 33:6, 9). The author of Hebrews echoes this teaching: "The worlds were framed by the word of God, so that things which are seen were not made of things which do appear" (Heb. 11:3).

(Biblical Creationism)

GOD

Ex Nihilo

Journalist Bruce Feiler devoted more than a year to investigating the biblical sites where some of the most important events in the Bible occurred. The following paragraph records the spiritual lessons he learned.

"By the end, I came to believe that the essential spirit that animates those places also animates me. If that spirit is God, then I found God in the course of my journey. If that spirit is life, then I found life. Part of me suspects that it's both and that neither can exist without the other. Either way, what I know for sure is that all I had to do to discover that spirit was not look or listen or taste or feel. All I had to do was *remember*, for what I was looking for I somehow already knew."

In Six Days

The Genesis account of creation eloquently affirms the power, wisdom, and authority of God by recording that the entire universe was formed in only six days. With majestic simplicity, Genesis 1 emphasizes the amazing brevity of God's creation throughout its account: "And the evening and the morning were the first day . . . second day . . . third day . . . fourth day . . . fifth day . . . sixth day" (Gen. 1:5, 8, 13, 19, 23, 31). While giving the Ten Commandments, God reiterated that His work of creation took only six days: "In six days the Lord made heaven and earth, the sea, and all that in them is" (Exod. 20:11).

Modern science has attacked this aspect of the Bible's account perhaps more than any other. Referring to geological and astronomical evidence, many maintain that the biblical account is not scientifically credible. *Geological evidence* indicates that the earth's surface is composed of many layers of sediment. Within these layers, fossilized plants, animals, and humans have been found. Geologists and biologists believe that each layer represents a different time period of great length. Together these layers supposedly indicate that the earth is approximately three billion years old. Modern science also points to *astronomical evidence*. Since we today are able to see the light from stars millions of light years away, it seems impossible for the universe to be only a few thousand years old—as the account in Genesis 1 indicates.

Through the years many believing scholars have attempted to reconcile science and the Bible by proposing the **gap theory.** This theory states that a gap of millions of years should be understood between Genesis 1:1 and 1:2. Genesis 1:1 is supposed to record God's original creation, which included the angels. When Lucifer rebelled (Isa. 14:12-15), God judged him and all who followed him, including the earth and its inhabitants. After bringing the earth to a chaotic ruin, God waited many millions of years before beginning a second creation, which is recorded in Genesis 1:2-31. God's judgment of the earth accounts for the geological evidence, and the long period of waiting explains how the light from stars millions of light-years away can now been seen from the earth.

The gap theory, however, assumes a great deal more about the wording of Genesis 1 than the context will allow. According to this view, one of the most important details regarding the origin of the universe has been omitted and must be inferred between the two opening verses of the Bible. Such a theory is more inventive than perceptive. If this approach to biblical interpretation were legitimate, we would wonder how many other doctrines are waiting to be discovered as hidden "gaps" between verses in the Bible. If such an approach were applied to the entire Bible, it would quickly become clear that the real authority would not be the Bible itself, but the Bible interpreter.

GAP THEORY

GENESIS 1:1					GENESIS 1:2-31
		MILLIONS OF YEARS			

DAY-AGE THEORY

MILLIONS OF YEARS	MILLIONS OF YEARS	MILLIONS OF YEARS	MILLIONS OF YEARS	MILLIONS OF YEARS	MILLIONS OF YEARS
DAY 1	DAY 2	DAY 3	DAY 4	DAY 5	DAY 6

Scholars have also proposed the **day-age theory,** which states that each creative day in Genesis 1 was actually a period of many millions of years. Proponents find support for this view from the fact that the Hebrew word for "day" *(yom)* can refer to time periods longer than twenty-four hours (Isa. 2:12; Ezek. 22:24). Accordingly, during each *yom* God did not create things instantaneously but rather worked in an evolutionary manner. He simply directed evolutionary processes so that by the end of each *yom* the substances/organisms mentioned in Genesis 1 were produced. Scholars refer to this theory of God's work as *theistic evolution.* Not only does this theory account for the geological and astronomical evidences, but it also accounts for them in a way that agrees with many of the explanations presented by Darwinian evolution.

The day-age theory should also be rejected. Although it is true that the Hebrew word *yom* can refer to a time period longer than a single day, it is normally used to refer to a twenty-four hour period. Furthermore, the context of Genesis 1 demands understanding *yom* as a twenty-four hour day. Throughout the account each *yom* is defined as a period consisting of "the evening and the morning" (Gen. 1:5, 8, 13, 19, 23, 31). Only a *yom* that is twenty-four hours long would comprise just one evening and one morning.

It seems best to interpret all the events in Genesis 1 as occurring within six literal days. Two observations indicate that this interpretation is compatible with the scientific data mentioned earlier. First, all the geological evidence seeming to indicate an old earth could have been produced by the *universal flood* of Genesis 6-8. The massive cataclysms involved in this divine judgment could have buried an entire world of humans, animals, and plants in different layers of sedimentary rock. Therefore, what geologists suppose has taken millions of years, could have taken place in a very short time. Second, in considering the astronomical evidence, we must remember that God created this world with *apparent age.* God made Adam and Eve as mature adults. He also created a garden full of trees that were bearing fruit only three days after being made. It is reasonable to conclude that He also created the heavens with apparent age. God not only created the stars themselves, but He also made the light emanating from them so that they could immediately "be for signs, and for seasons, and for days and years" as a help and guide to His earthly creatures (Gen. 1:14).

Originally Good

Five times the biblical account tells us that what God made was good (Gen. 1:10, 12, 18, 21, 25). And once man was created, the narrative concludes, "God saw every thing that he had made,

Think About It!

The Bible clearly teaches that God made His world "very good." This repeated emphasis in the Genesis account of creation presents a significant problem for those who believe in theistic evolution. Can you discern what that problem is?

and, behold, it was very good" (v. 31). This emphasis indicates that evil is not eternal but that it entered the world at some point after creation. It also indicates that the physical world is not inherently bad. Realizing that matter is not evil is essential to helping us shun the harmful tendencies of *asceticism,* which teaches that spirituality is gained through depriving oneself of material comforts. There is nothing inherently sinful about enjoying good food or other physical pleasures. We do wrong only if we use these things in a sinful way. As Paul taught, God created a world of pleasures "to be received with thanksgiving of them which believe and know the truth. For every creature of God is good, and nothing to be refused, if it be received with thanksgiving: for it is sanctified by the word of God and prayer" (I Tim. 4:3-5).

Ongoing

Although God's initial creation was accomplished *ex nihilo,* much of His subsequent creation was produced using existing

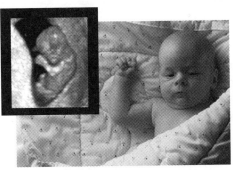

The greatest marvel of the world's first week is a marvel that continues to this day.

matter. Vegetation was produced from the earth (Gen. 1:12), and man's body was formed "of the dust of the ground" (Gen. 2:7). Nevertheless, plant life and human life were no less God's creation than His original work. Just as God used existing matter in that first week of the earth's existence, so also He continues to use existing materials in His ongoing creative work. One area in which God continues His creative work is in the realm of human procreation. David praises God for being his Maker in Psalm 139. God was so intimately involved in every

Think About It!

As we consider God's ongoing creative work, we are naturally drawn to consider the abortion controversy. Read the following quotation. Using what the Bible says about creation, can you formulate an answer to the writer's doubts regarding the personhood of the unborn?

"One traditional antiabortion argument has centered on pointing out the many ways in which a fetus resembles a baby. They emphasize its development ('It already has ten fingers . . .') without mentioning its dissimilarities to adults (it still has gills and a tail). . . . Historically, the time at which a person has been said to come into existence has varied widely. . . . Nor is this variety of opinions surprising. Biologically, a human being develops gradually. We shouldn't expect there to be any specific time or sharp dividing point when a person appears on the scene."

stage of David's fetal development that he could say, "Thou hast covered me in my mother's womb" (v. 13). All of us are the creation of God. The means by which He made Adam and Eve is different than the means He used to make us, but we are no less the work of His hands. We with David may rejoice in God's love and concern for us from the moment of our conception: "Thine eyes did see my substance, yet being unperfect; and in thy book all my members were written, which in continuance were fashioned, when as yet there was none of them" (Ps. 139:16).

Implications from the Biblical Evidence

Rejection of Evolution

The biblical presentation of the origin of the universe leaves no room for Darwinian evolution. Darwin's theory has basically two tenets. First, all species are linked together through a long period of development that eventually can be traced back to one original cell. Second, this development—which accounts for all biological diversity among the species—takes place randomly. Whereas Genesis states that creation took place in six days, Darwin states that it took place over millions of years. Whereas Genesis records that God made individual organisms to reproduce "after their kind" (Gen. 1:21), Darwin claims that all species are derived ultimately from a single one-cell organism. And whereas Genesis attributes the existence of all life to the direct working of God, Darwin attempts to account for the existence of all things by the work of a random natural process. It is hard to imagine a theory more at variance with the biblical account of the origin of the universe than Darwinian evolution.

Divine Ownership

God created the universe as a free act of His own will; therefore, the world belongs to Him. As David said, "The earth is the Lord's, and the fulness thereof; the world, and they that dwell therein. For he hath founded it upon the seas, and established it upon the floods" (Ps. 24:1-2). Since God owns us body and soul, we are not free to choose our own way in life. Not even the Athenians that Paul addressed on Mars' Hill were free from God's claim on them. Even though they knew nothing of the Bible, Paul asserted that they were to "seek the Lord" (Acts 17:27). If the heathen in ancient Greece were obligated to find God's will and do it, how much more are we obligated as professing Christians? This obligation is not something that can be safely ignored. As Paul warned those Greeks, "[God] hath appointed a day, in the which he will judge the world in righteousness" (Acts 17:31). What does this God expect from His creatures? In a phrase, *total devotion*. One of the most important manifestations of that devotion is praise from a sincere heart: "Know ye that the Lord he is God: it is he that hath made us, and not we ourselves; we are his people. . . . Enter into his gates with thanksgiving, and into his courts with praise: be thankful unto him, and bless his name" (Ps. 100:3-4).

God's Care for Man

From beginning to end God's special care for man is demonstrated by the biblical account of creation. It is significant that God did not make Adam until the final day of creation. Only after He had richly furnished the earth with countless good things, did God form man from the dust of the ground. Thus the first man was not exposed to a single moment of deprivation or difficulty. God's care is also seen in the perspective maintained throughout the creation account. Everything in Genesis 1-2 is told from the viewpoint of man's benefit. Even the heavens, seemingly infinite in their scope, are said to be made for man: "Let them be for signs, and for seasons, and for days and years" (Gen. 1:14). Another evidence of God's concern for man is the fact that the climax of Genesis 1 is not the glory of the majestic deep or the staggering expanse of outer space. God's greatest creation is man. Four times in two verses, the text states that God made man in His own image. And whereas the text gives only five *words* to God's creation of the galaxies (Gen. 1:16), it takes five *verses*—and all of the next chapter—to describe the creation of man.

Finally, the biblical account emphasizes God's care for man by stating that God concluded the week of creation with a day of rest: "God blessed the seventh day, and sanctified it: because that in it he had rested from all his work" (Gen. 2:3). As the Bible later records, this sanctified day was for man (Mark 2:27). God not only richly furnished His world to meet man's physical needs, but He also programmed the rhythms of each week so that His highest creation might enjoy regular refreshment. Moses later explains that this sanctified time amounts to more than simply a day without work. It should be a time to remember God's goodness and love: "Remember that thou wast a servant in the land of Egypt, and that the Lord thy God brought thee out thence through a mighty hand and by a stretched out arm: therefore the Lord thy God commanded thee to keep the sabbath day" (Deut. 5:15).

Divine Revelation

"The heavens declare the glory of God; and the firmament sheweth his handywork" (Ps. 19:1). Like the invention of a skilled engineer or the symphony of an accomplished musician, the universe reveals its Maker. Although we could note hundreds of

things that nature reveals about God, two observations at this point must suffice. First, creation tells those willing to listen that God is a God of beauty. The brilliant bursts of a sunset, the elegant purity of the midnight moon, the breathtaking colors of

"For Glory and for Beauty"

Have you ever seen the exclamation, "Jesus loves you so much it hurt!"? The expression is true enough, but it communicates one of the deepest truths known to mankind in a very light, almost flippant, way. The hymn printed below, however, expresses Christ's amazing love much more appropriately. Its elevated beauty is more suitable as a prayer to our beauty-loving God, and its wording comes closer to capturing the profundity of Christ's sacrifice.

O sacred Head, now wounded,
With grief and shame weighed
   down,
Now scornfully surrounded
With thorns, Thine only crown;
O sacred Head, what glory,
What bliss till now was Thine!
Yet, though despised and gory,
I joy to call Thee mine.

What Thou, my Lord, hast suffered
Was all for sinner's gain:
Mine, mine was the transgression,
But Thine the deadly pain;
Lo, here I fall, my Savior!
'Tis I deserve Thy place;
Look on me with Thy favor,
Vouch-safe to me Thy grace.

trees in autumn, the majesty of snowcapped mountain peaks, and the tickling rhythms of a little child's laugh are all woven together into a tapestry of exquisite beauty. Surely the God who made such a world delights in beauty, and surely we—who bear His image— should delight in it as well. We should take time to enjoy and reflect on the beauties of God's world. We also should give effort to learning how to praise our beautiful God in a beautiful way. This is a skill that previous generations of the Christian church were much better at than we are. Our generation has so labored to make God and His praises "relevant" that it has nearly lost the ability to extol God's greatness and goodness with the beauty that is appropriate to His being. Just as the Old Testament priests were to present themselves before the Lord wearing beautiful garments, so also we should endeavor to fashion our praises "for glory and for beauty" (Exod. 28:2).

Second, creation reminds us that God's mind is infinite. The God who could design, construct, and enliven an infinitely complex world with only the words "Let there be" is surely Himself infinite.

The remarkably complex structure of this giant Amazon lily pad represents only a small fraction of all that came into existence when God simply commanded, "Let the earth bring forth" (Gen. 1:11).

As finite beings, we sometimes wonder how God could run the universe and still pay attention to us or hear our prayers. When, however, we consider what all God did in six days several thousand years ago, we quickly realize that there is plenty of room in the mind of God for every one of our prayers, thoughts, and concerns. Although our minds are not big enough to be constantly occupied with Him, His mind can be constantly occupied with us—and it is (Ps. 139:17-18).

God's Work of Providence

Some of our early American leaders—including Benjamin Franklin, Thomas Jefferson, Ethan Allen, and Thomas Paine—held to a belief called *deism*. They claimed that God created the world but then stepped back and let it operate without supernatural intervention. To them, people who viewed God as directly involved in this world were superstitious. They preferred to think of God as a cosmic watchmaker, who crafted the universe, wound it up, and then left it to run according to His design. Although believing in God's direct involvement in the world may seem superstitious to some, the Bible clearly teaches that God is *sovereign,* that He exercises supreme and permanent authority over His world. The God of the Bible not only made the world, but He also remains active in all that happens. This continuing work of God in the world is called God's *providence*. Through the centuries, theologians have identified two particular manifestations of God's providence: preservation and government.

The most significant challenge to deism in Scripture is the birth of Jesus Christ. The fact that God came to earth as a man and lived among His creatures for over three decades shatters the image of a distant deity. It should come as no surprise, therefore, that Benjamin Franklin did not believe in Christ's deity. As the following excerpt from a letter he wrote late in life indicates, this founding father ended his days rejecting one of the central tenets of Christian theology.

"As to Jesus of Nazareth, my Opinion of whom you particularly desire, I think the System of Morals and his Religion, as he left them to us, the best the World ever saw or is likely to see; but I apprehend it has received various corrupting Changes, and I have . . . some Doubts as to his Divinity; tho' it is a question I do not dogmatize upon, having never studied it, and think it needless to busy myself with it now, when I expect soon an Opportunity of knowing the Truth with less Trouble. I see no harm, however, in its being believed, if that Belief has the good Consequence as probably it has, of making his Doctrines more respected and better observed."

Divine Preservation

"Thou hast made heaven, the heaven of heavens, with all their host, the earth, and all things that are therein . . . and thou preservest them all" (Neh. 9:6). God's *preservation* refers to His continuing work of sustaining all that He has created. God preserves His world, first of all, by holding the entire material universe together. He is the reason that atomic particles cohere and that chemical compounds do not break apart chaotically. Speaking of Christ, Paul states, "He is before all things, and by him all things consist [hold together]" (Col. 1:17; see also Heb. 1:3). Scripture also indicates that God preserves His creation by daily supplying its needs. The psalmist reflects on God's tender care for His creatures in Psalm 104:

"He sendeth the springs into the valleys, which run among the hills. They give drink to every beast of the field. . . . He watereth the hills from his chambers: the earth is satisfied with the fruit of thy works" (vv. 10-11, 13).

It should be plain from these verses that nothing in God's creation is self-sufficient. Indeed, every one of us can echo the words of David: "The eyes of all wait upon thee; and thou givest them their meat in due season" (Ps. 145:15). When we consider what the Bible teaches regarding God's preservation, we begin to understand the importance of cultivating a grateful spirit. The food we eat, the clothes we wear, the health we enjoy, and the air we breathe are all gifts from the hand of God. Remembering God's preservation should also encourage us in times of difficulty. When we are unable to pay our bills, when we lose our health, or when we feel we have no strength to continue bearing our burdens, the thought of God's preserving work can refresh our spirits. Our loving, all-wise God is the keeper of all good things, and He delights in proving true the words of Paul: "My God shall supply all your need according to his riches in glory by Christ Jesus" (Phil. 4:19).

Divine Government

Divine government refers to the work of God by which He directs the entire universe to the conclusion that He has purposed for it. God's preservation is retrospective in its orientation; it concerns

Think About It!

As secular humanists, the signers of *Humanist Manifesto 2000* believe either that God does not exist or that He is not relevant to human life. Such a belief certainly gives one a feeling of great independence and freedom from eternal accountability. That feeling, however, comes at a price—as the following excerpts demonstrate.

"We urge today, as in the past, that humans not look beyond themselves for salvation. We alone are responsible for our own destiny, and the best we can do is to muster our intelligence, courage, and compassion to realize our highest aspirations."

"Global environmental problems must be dealt with at the planetary level: reducing environmental pollution, including carbon dioxide and other greenhouse gases; developing alternative fuels; reforesting denuded lands . . . protecting endangered species; reducing the addictive lifestyle of conspicuous wasteful consumption; and banning all weapons of mass destruction. Measures to protect the environment thus need high priority for the planetary community."

the divine activity of maintaining the world as it has been. God's government, however, has a future orientation. It is God's work of guiding the world toward its consummation.

The Extent of God's Governing Work

The Bible teaches that God rules over all the events in **nature.** In the Psalms God is presented as the controller of natural forces: "Whatsoever the Lord pleased, that did he in heaven, and in earth, in the seas, and all the deep places. He causeth the vapours to ascend from the ends of the earth; he maketh lightnings for the rain; he bringeth the wind out of his treasuries" (Ps. 135:6-7). The animal kingdom is also under God's rule. Ravens brought food to Elijah because of God's command (I Kings 17:4), serpents afflicted the rebellious Israelites by divine decree (Num. 21:6), and Daniel was saved from the lions because God had "shut the lions' mouths" (Dan. 6:22). From the ebbing of the tides (Job 38:8-11) to the death of each sparrow (Matt. 10:29), God is the ruler over the natural world.

God's sovereign rule also includes the rise and fall of the **nations of the earth.** This aspect of divine government is one of the central themes in the Book of Daniel. Daniel's remarkable accounts, written to the Judeans in exile, assure God's people that their Lord is indeed the King of kings. In one vision God reveals that the great empires of the earth are simply precursors of God's indomitable kingdom. One day that kingdom will come to earth and "break in pieces and consume all these kingdoms [of men], and it shall stand for ever" (Dan. 2:44). The fourth chapter of Daniel was actually written by Nebuchadnezzar, the most power-ful man on earth at the time (sixth century B.C.). As emperor of Babylon's vast kingdom, this man records how the God of Israel humiliated him and taught him that the real ruler over each nation is God, not man. "The most High ruleth in the kingdom of men, and giveth it to whomsoever he will, and setteth up over it the basest of men. . . . I Nebuchadnezzar lifted up mine eyes unto heaven . . . and I praised and honoured him . . . whose dominion is an everlasting dominion, and his kingdom is from generation to generation" (Dan. 4:17, 34).

The **choices of individuals** are also included in God's rule. Cyrus's decision to send the Jews back to their homeland was in fact God's decision (II Chron. 36:22-23; Isa. 44:28). The disciples' choice to follow Christ was predetermined by the Father (John 17:2, 6, 9). Those who chose to accept the gospel preached by Paul and Barnabas had been supernaturally "ordained to eternal life" (Acts 13:48). And Paul taught that the good works that we as Christians choose each day "God hath before ordained that we should walk in them" (Eph. 2:10).

This divine government also encompasses the evil choices of men and women. Judas's choice to betray Christ, the chief priests' choice to accuse Him, and Pilate's choice to let Him die innocently were all God's chosen means "to do whatsoever thy hand and thy counsel determined before to be done" (Acts 4:28; 2:23; Luke 22:22). The life of Joseph is perhaps the most impressive example of God's working through the evil choices of others. Filled with hatred, Joseph's brothers sold him into slavery when he was only seventeen. After many difficult trials, Joseph rose to prominence and eventually became the second most powerful man in Egypt. When the brothers learned that the boy they had sold as a slave had become one of Egypt's chief rulers, they feared for their lives. Joseph forgave them, however, and shared

If a good God is in control of all that happens in the world, why do bad things happen? The following quotation represents one theologian's attempt to reconcile what the Bible reveals about God and the reality of evil. Is it truth or error?

"In the last judgment the problem of evil will be solved; yet on the road that leads to the last judgment the workings of providence doubtless will remain something of a mystery to us. Our finite minds are simply unable to conceive the wisdom of this infinite process in which we live and move. Faith in divine providence calls the believer to walk without seeing, based on what is known from God's disclosure in Christ."

EXAMINE THE CONTEXT   Read Acts 2:23 and Luke 22:22 in context. God did foreordain the betrayal of His Son and the injustice that He received in the Jewish courts. However, what does the broader context of these verses teach us about those involved in this betrayal and injustice?

with them a lesson that he had learned regarding God's providential government: "Be not grieved, nor angry with yourselves, that ye sold me hither: for God did send me" (Gen. 45:5). God's plan for the ages cannot be frustrated by the sinful choices of His creatures. Ultimately, even sin accomplishes God's will.

After considering this evidence, we should not be surprised by Paul's description of God's rule over the world: "[God] worketh all things after the counsel of his own will" (Eph. 1:11). When we ask what exactly is part of God's governing activity, Scripture gives us an assuring answer—*everything.*

The Purpose of God's Governing Work

The ultimate purpose of God's sovereign rule is to glorify Himself. All that happens in the universe is working together to declare that God is unique and that He in His greatness and His goodness infinitely excels everything else that exists. When the Lord delivered His people from captivity, He explained, "I do not this for your sakes, O house of Israel, but for mine holy name's sake. . . . I will sanctify [set apart] my great name" (Ezek. 36:22-23). In the New Testament, Paul states that the world is ordered as it is so that "in all things he [Jesus Christ] might have the preeminence" (Col. 1:18). And in Romans the apostle expresses the ultimate purpose of God's working with eloquent brevity: "Of him, and through him, and to him, are all things: to whom be glory for ever. Amen" (Rom. 11:36).

God's glory is the most general expression of the purpose of the divine plan. In various places, Scripture reveals this purpose more specifically, and perhaps the best example of a more specific statement is found in Ephesians 1:10. Here Paul states that God is at work in the world so that one day "he might gather together in one all things in Christ, both which are in heaven, and which are on earth; even in him." God has chosen to glorify

Himself supremely through the work of His Son. All that happens in nature, all that believers do, and all that the wicked attempt to do is working together to usher in the full kingship of Jesus Christ. One day Christ the Lord will return to earth and set up a kingdom that will completely subject all things that "are in heaven, and which are on the earth" under His authority. Speaking of this glorious day, Paul, in another place, states the reason that Christ's kingdom is essential to the Father's plan: "When all things shall be subdued unto [Christ], then shall the Son also himself be subject unto him that put all things under him, that God may be all in all" (I Cor. 15:28). God the Father has planned out all that happens in order to bring about the kingdom of His Son, and He is establishing this kingdom in order to make Himself "all in all" through His Son.

GOD HAS PLANNED...

ALL THAT HAPPENS...

TO ESTABLISH CHRIST'S KINGDOM...

TO GLORIFY HIMSELF

The Father, the Son, a glorious kingdom, heaven and earth—where do *we* fit in? The apostle John reveals that when Christ returns, "we shall be like him; for we shall see him as he is" (I John 3:2). For this reason, Peter could say in his second epistle that those who know the Lord will one day be "partakers of the divine nature" (II Pet. 1:4). Of course, we will never be like Christ in His deity, His infinity, or His uniqueness. We will, however, share in His righteousness, purity, truth, and immortality. Loosed from the chains of sin and earth, we will shine in Christ's eternal kingdom as living, breathing proclamations of His moral perfections.

God has a plan for each of us, and when His Son returns that plan will be perfected, a plan that was fashioned long before any of us were born. God has called us to declare His eternal praise by bearing in our glorified bodies the likeness of His Son. "Whom he did foreknow, he also did predestinate to be conformed to the image of his Son, that he [the Son] might be the firstborn among many brethren" (Rom. 8:29). The fact that God's greatest concern is for His own glory should only encourage us as believers.

What Would You Say?

Our consideration of God's governing work naturally leads to a difficult question: *How can God control all that happens and human beings still be free to choose what they will do?* Based on what you know of the Bible's teaching, can you answer this question?

By glorifying Himself, God serves the best interests of each Christian. Because God has determined to glorify His Son through our glorification and glorify Himself through His Son, we can find comfort in Paul's profound assurance: "All things work together for good to them that love God, to them who are the called according to his purpose" (Rom. 8:28).

God's Special Providence—Miracles

Normally, God's providence operates through the usual patterns of nature. At times, however, God works not through nature but in spite of it. This special providence that interrupts the usual patterns of nature is called a *miracle*. God worked a miracle through Moses when he stood before Pharaoh and threw down his rod. Contrary to nature, the wood was transformed into the tissues of a living serpent (Exod. 7:10). When one of Elisha's fellow prophets lost an axe head in the Jordan River, God worked a miracle by causing it to float (II Kings 6:6). God's supernatural power overruled the natural pattern of iron sinking in water. Likewise, Christ worked a miracle by giving sight to a man who ha d been blind from birth (John 9:6-7). Retinas that had never reacted properly to light waves and nerve cells that had never conducted impulses corrected themselves instantly and began functioning as though they had never been flawed.

Frequently in Scripture God employs this special work to accomplish two purposes. God does miracles, first of all, to meet human needs. This purpose was particularly common during Jesus' earthly ministry, which was characterized by compassionate supernatural deeds designed to relieve human suffering. It seems clear from Scripture, however, that each of these deeds also served a higher purpose, a purpose that directs every miracle—*divine testimony.* God does the miraculous to verify that an accompanying revelation is true and divine in its origin. Historically, most miracles have taken place either during the ministries of Moses and Joshua, Elijah and Elisha, or Jesus and the apostles. In each period the supernatural works were designed to convince those who saw them that God was indeed at work and that the message that these men spoke was from God. Jesus taught this interpretation of His miracles when He compared them to the testimony of John the Baptist: "I have greater witness than that of John: for the works which the Father hath given me to finish, the same works that I do, bear witness of me, that the Father hath sent me" (John 5:36).

As we consider this special work of God's providence, it is only natural for us to wonder whether we may expect miracles today. Scripture seems to indicate that we may—*if we keep the right purposes in mind.* The Bible condemns those who seek a miracle

God has verified His revelation to mankind through miracles. Amazingly, however, those very miracles have become a stumbling block, keeping many people from believing God's Word. Harry Emerson Fosdick, a famous liberal preacher of the early twentieth century, was such a man. He labored for many years attempting to convince church members that the Bible's miraculous accounts were untrue. He once wrote in a book, "To suppose that a man in order to be a loyal and devout disciple of our Lord in the twentieth century A.D. must think that God in the ninth century B.C. miraculously . . . made an axe-head swim seems to me dangerously ridiculous. . . . Certainly, I find some of the miracle-narratives of Scripture historically incredible." Such unbelief in the face of many wonderful divine validations is one of the most condemning ironies in human history.

to satisfy skepticism (Matt. 16:1-4), idle curiosity (Luke 23:8), or a desire for fame and power (Acts 8:19-22). However, there is no biblical evidence that God will not work a miracle today to relieve suffering or to verify His presence and work in the world. One day each of us will kneel beside the bed of a loved one whose suffering is beyond the skill of doctors. In that hour we should remember that the same Lord who healed the sick and gave sight to the blind hears the prayers of believers. If we pray with the right purposes in mind, God may choose to glorify Himself through a special manifestation of His providence (James 5:14-15). But even if our worst fears are realized, Christ has promised, "I am the resurrection, and the life: he that believeth in me, though he were dead, yet shall he live" (John 11:25). Though in God's good and all-wise providence the miracle of healing may not be ours, the miracle of resurrection is certain for all believers. Confidently expecting this miracle is no superstitious fancy. It is fundamental to biblical Christianity. If there is no coming resurrection, there is no Christianity—"But thanks be to God, which giveth us the victory through our Lord Jesus Christ" (I Cor. 15:57).

Conclusion

God is at work in the world through every event and situation. Though His deeds often mystify us, Scripture assures us that the goal to which He is working all things will accomplish His own glory and our highest good. Many difficult turns in the road are ahead for each of us. We must always remember, however, that His wise and gracious hand has ordered every step of the way. What lies before us is the best path to the best end.

God Moves in a Mysterious Way
William Cowper, 1731-1800

God moves in a mysterious way
His wonders to perform;
He plants His footsteps in the sea,
And rides upon the storm.

Ye fearful saints, fresh courage take;
The clouds ye so much dread
Are big with mercy, and shall break
In blessings on your head.

Judge not the Lord by feeble sense,
But trust Him for His grace;
Behind a frowning providence
He hides a smiling face.

His purposes will ripen fast,
Unfolding every hour:
The bud may have a bitter taste,
But sweet will be the flower.

Blind unbelief is sure to err,
And scan His work in vain:
God is His own interpreter,
And He will make it plain.

CHAPTER THREE

In the Image of God

3

Memory Verses: Genesis 1:26-27; Romans 5:12

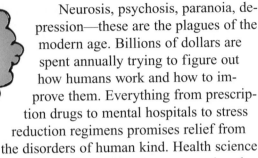

WHO ARE WE?
WHY ARE WE
LIKE WE ARE?

Neurosis, psychosis, paranoia, depression—these are the plagues of the modern age. Billions of dollars are spent annually trying to figure out how humans work and how to improve them. Everything from prescription drugs to mental hospitals to stress reduction regimens promises relief from the disorders of human kind. Health science is useful to a degree, but it never reaches the roots of our problems.

Who are we and why are we like we are? Though human beings have conceived many wrong answers to these questions, God has provided the answer in the plainest language possible. The Bible tells what man is like and what is wrong with him. The answer is simple to understand but very difficult to accept.

In the first two chapters you read about God Himself. Now you are going to consider what God revealed about mankind and how we came to our present relationship with God. It is here that we study the origin of the problem between God and man. In later chapters, we will look at the person and work of Jesus Christ, who solved that problem.

The Scripture teaches two general truths about humanity. First, God created man as a pure and holy being with exceptionally high

GET THE BIG

PICTURE

I. God Created Man to Reflect His Glory
 A. The Image of God
 B. The Constitution of the Human Race
II. Man Rebelled Against God
 A. The Temptation and First Sin of Man
 B. The Nature of Sin

honor. Second, man rebelled against God, ruining his holiness and losing himself to the power of sin. This chapter studies the biblical revelation of man according to those two truths.

God Created Man to Reflect His Glory

Our first object is to see in Scripture what God intended for man to be. Man was to be a perfect reflection of God's glory. Individual men, individual women, and the human race corporately all reflect God's glory in different ways. God's glory is greater than man can reflect, of course, but to the extent man can show God's glory, he showed it flawlessly, or perfectly.

There are two aspects to the creation of man that we must take into account: the creation of man in God's image and the constitution (composition or make-up) of man. Understanding both of these aspects together enables you to realize what you and everyone around you could have been, *should* have been, and can be yet again.

Our scriptural information is based on the first two chapters of Genesis. The first chapter of Genesis describes Creation from a broad, cosmic viewpoint. It includes the creation and blessing of the first humans as its climax. The second chapter of Genesis "zooms in" on the creation of man and retells it with greater detail. These two chapters form the foundation for a study of what man was like as God originally made him.

Genesis 1:26-28 and 2:4-25 are the two passages in Genesis that record the creation of man. We will examine each of these chapters to see what man was as God made him before he sinned.

Think About It!

Whoever you are, everything in this chapter affects you personally. While we are nowhere told what life would have been like if our first parents had never sinned, we know that all of the hardship and sorrow in life springs from their sin. But much better, you can see what God still intends for you to be. As you read this chapter, contemplate such questions as the following:

What is the ideal relationship between man and woman?
What was life like when everyone was perfect?
What did we lose as a result of the first sin?

In the Hebrew language of the Old Testament, *man* was used to refer to the human race as a whole. The word does not reflect gender bias, as Genesis 1:27 makes clear when it uses the words *man* and *him*, made in God's image, and then clarifies that He created them *male* and *female*. Often, too much is made of the differences between men and women and not enough of their similarities as humans.

The Image of God

What exactly does it mean that you and I are made in God's image? To be in the image of God is the essence of what it is to be human. We will first examine the word *image* and attempt to understand its significance. Then we will look at an analogy from Scripture for the meaning of the phrase "image of God." Finally we will look closely at the phrase in its context in Genesis 1.

The Creation of Man

Genesis 1 places the creation of man after the creation of everything else and devotes to it five verses, more than to any other part of Creation. God's introductory phrase is "Let us make man in our image." We have two questions to address: who is the "us" in this sentence, and what does this phrase tell us about the image of God?

The Lord spoke as if He were including someone else when He said, "Let us make man in our image." There are three common explanations for the plural.

First, God was talking to the holy angels. This is not likely because angels are not equal in power to God and man is never said to be in the image of angels.

Second, God was speaking in the plural to express His majesty. Ancient kings of the past and European kings today speak as if they were plural in order to express their royal importance. Also, Hebrew uses the form of the plural to express intensity or grandeur, even when a numeric plural is not in consideration. Nevertheless, this explanation isn't certain because God refers to Himself in this way only one other time (Gen. 11:7).

Third, God was speaking as the Trinity. But this view is weak because the Trinity is not made clear for a long time and because there is no other mention of man's being in the image of the Trinity.

Overall, the second option is best, but it is good to remain open-minded about this verse.

Image Illustration

God the Creator made man as the crown of Creation. He uses two words to describe the relationship of man to God, usually translated *image* and *likeness*. These two words probably are two ways of saying the same thing, especially since the next verse uses just the first word to reiterate the same event.

Image or *likeness* is used for something stamped from a mold. The word *model* is a good modern equivalent. Likewise a photograph or a video recording is an illustration of the same concept. A model airplane is the image and likeness of the real airplane it is based on. You keep a photo of your best friend to remind you of her. The photo is not your friend, but it looks like her and its sole purpose is to represent her and to bring her to mind when she is elsewhere.

Imagine you become friends with a married couple who attend your church. They are kind and loving to each other and always praising one another in public. Suppose their names are Mike and Macy.

One day, you and a couple of others from church are at their new house helping them get some work done. Mike is gone on some errands and you haven't seen Macy for a while. You happen to walk into their living room and see Macy shredding an 8" x 10" portrait of Mike. Startled, she looks up, sees you, and lays the torn picture facedown on the coffee table.

"Macy, are you mad at Mike?" you ask sincerely.

"Oh, no! Not at all," Macy replies. "I adore Mike. What makes you ask a question like that?" Then she picks up his picture and resumes ripping and crumpling it.

Do you believe her?

It makes no sense for Macy to treat Mike's image in any way that does not reflect her feelings toward Mike. Whether she keeps his picture in her purse, frames it in her house, or tears it up and burns it, she is reflecting her attitude toward Mike himself.

We can use this illustration to get some idea of what it means that man is made in God's image. How we treat a "picture" of God reflects our feelings toward and our relationship to Him. Abusing and degrading God's image shows scorn for God. Caring for and exalting God's image manifests love and appreciation for God. Whether we abuse ourselves or other people, we deface the image of God.

An Inspired Analogy

An analogy God has given us to help understand the image of God is our children. Genesis 5:3 says that Adam fathered a son, Seth, in his own image and likeness. Scripture uses the same words to describe how Adam was in the image and likeness of God. You know that children look like their parents and grandparents and usually act like them, too. Even if you wish you didn't look or act like Mom or Dad, you cannot help it. When you have your own family and children, you'll realize more than ever how much of your parents is in you. Furthermore, you'll see yourself reflected in your own kids, both good and bad.

Context

Context is always our best guide in determining what a word or sentence means. In Genesis 1:26 God immediately links the creation of man in His image with man's dominion over the rest of animate creation. *Dominion* means the right to rule. God gave man, both male and female, the right to rule all other living creatures. Evidently we should consider dominion a major component of the image of God. It is not all there is to the image, but it is a good control for analyzing other components of meaning in "the image of God."

IMAGE OF GOD

•**Dominion**
•**Intelligence**
•**Morality**

By a *control* we mean something that prevents our straying too far from the biblical text by heaping up implications. You have probably learned that students of the Scripture should be careful when they make conclusions based on what the Bible says. Defining the image of God is one area in which some scholars have made more conclusions than the Bible warrants, adding more components than are really there.

To see the importance of restraining our interpretations, let's consider a few things that the image of God is not. It is not that man reflects the Trinity of God by being a little trinity of his own. (See "The Elements of a Human Being" below.) It is not an indication that God imparted some of Himself to make us, and now we are all a little bit God. That is pantheism, and it is unscriptural. The image is also not equivalent to the physical body of man, for John 4:24 tells us plainly that God is Spirit. He does not have a body with arms and legs that He used as a prototype for the first man.

What then is the image of God? Since dominion is one element, it appears that we mirror God's function as ruler. Like Him, we rule. We don't rule the same things He does, for God rules all the universe, spiritual and physical. Man under God rules over a part of the universe, a part over which God gave him dominion.

It may be that the image of God involves those ways in which human relations to the natural world reflect God's relationship to the world. Examples would be the way we utilize the world (as the first man and woman were to tend the Garden of Eden) and rule animals (Adam named all animals). Involved in these actions are human intelligence and will. Therefore we may conclude that God's image included the importation of our rational intellect, will, and moral nature.

The Constitution of the Human Race

At this point we turn to consider what man actually is. In our study of how man reflects God's glory, we have established that man is made in the image of God. The image includes man's dominion over nature, his intelligence, his will, and his spiritual/moral being. But what is man made up of? Are there multiple parts to a human being? The extraordinary physical and spiritual complexity of a human being manifests God's glory as a wise and precise Creator.

The Elements of a Human Being

First, we consider whether or not a human being can be subdivided into different parts. You need to know what parts there are to you. Some modern scientists want you to believe that you are just a mass of chemical processes, your self-consciousness nothing but a steady sequence of electrical impulses. Does the Bible say differently? If so, how should it affect the way you think and act?

Genesis 2 records a two-step process in God's creation of Adam, the first human being (*adam* is the Hebrew word for man or humanity, so to say "God created Adam" is the same as to say "God created man.") Read Genesis 2:7. The first step was forming man out of dirt. The second step was breathing into the nostrils of man the breath of life. Thus the body made from dirt was not living, but it is called *man,* not just "the body" of man or "the flesh" of man.

Obviously, we don't have medical details about the precision of God's sculpting of the first man's body. The "breath of life" is the miraculous power that created life where there had been no life. The last clause of verse 7 says only that man became a *living being,* or *soul*—a generic term, not distinguishing man from living animals. Therefore, Genesis 2:7 does not give direct evidence for a subdivision of a human being. It presents the man as a singular, unified entity, though the body and life are created in two distinct stages.

B O D Y & S O U L

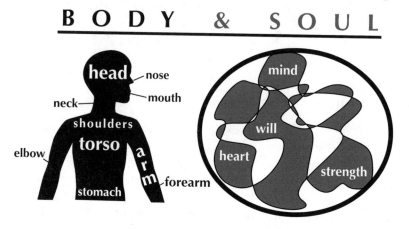

However, when we survey the rest of the Bible for indications of the subdivisions of man, we do find some evidence. Look at the six passages in the box below and consider how many parts a human appears to have according to them.

Does a human being consist of two, three, or four parts? Can it be that the passages don't necessarily overlap, so the total number of parts can be even more than four? This is confusing data, so we need to do a more careful analysis.

First, notice that several of these verses break up the "inner man," the part that isn't physical. Apparently, there are different ways to split it up. It is something like the way the physical body divides into arms, legs, head, heart, liver, and so forth. In fact, both the body and the spirit appear to be divisible into any number of parts. Therefore, it appears to be best to say that man can

Passages Teaching the Subdivision of Man

Genesis 1:26-27	1 part
Genesis 2:7	2 parts
Ecclesiastes 12:7	2 parts
I Thessalonians 5:23	3 parts
Hebrews 4:12	3 or 4 parts (?)
Luke 10:27	4 parts

be divided into two "parts," physical and spiritual, that either of these can be further subdivided an indefinite number of times, but that the biblical emphasis is on the fact that man is principally a unity. Man is incomplete without both physical and spiritual parts. The body does not live separately from the spirit nor does the spirit exist separately from the body, at least not forever.

The bottom line is that every human being is a fusion of both physical and spiritual being. We must avoid errors in emphasizing either one at the expense of the other. You are not just a body, just the sum of chemical processes, without an immaterial soul. But neither are you just a spirit trapped in a physical body; your body is bound to your soul, it is good, and you will have a body for eternity.

There are a few important applications to note here. One is that neither asceticism nor hedonism is scriptural. **Asceticism** is the idea that the physical body is evil and therefore it is right to abstain from physical pleasure. **Hedonism** is the idea that pleasure is inherently good and that therefore people should indulge in as much physical pleasure as possible. Both of these errors lead to ruin without improving a man's spiritual state.

Another application is that we cannot absolutely isolate physical from spiritual disorders. The spirit affects the body and the body affects the spirit. Sickness, injury, and disability can affect your spiritual state—they can literally make you more prone to sins like anger and bitterness. On the other hand, spiritual "diseases" like depression or guilt can harm the body. We must not overlook either cause, and we must not be misled by symptoms in one area to miss problems in the other one.

For example, you could find yourself suffering from continual bad moods and irritability. While it may be (and most likely is) a problem you need to correct spiritually, it is possible that the cause is medical, such as a slow-acting virus, eye trouble, or even an ear infection. To reverse the scenario, you may suffer from frequent headaches and stomach pain as a result of stress caused by worry over things you cannot control, which is a sin. This marks a spiritual problem that medicine will never cure, however much it may cover up the symptoms. You have to take into account the constitution of man as an integrated spiritual/physical being in order to understand illness.

Whoa, Man!

We need to take a special look at the creation of woman to complete our view of corporate humanity. Most of what we say about man applies to men and women equally, but there are differing details given to us in the creation of the first woman that are instructive to us today.

Genesis 1 combined the creation of the male and female humans as the single creation of man. Chapter 2 details creation, revealing that the male, or *man* ("Adam"), was created first and charged with keeping the Garden of Eden and avoiding one particular tree in the Garden, the tree of the knowledge of good and evil. Genesis 2:18 records God's remark that it is not good for man to be alone and His resolution to make for man a suitable assistant.

Significantly, God took flesh from Adam to make the first woman. When Adam saw her, he spoke a poem that is utterly beautiful in both form and meaning:

"This is now bone of my bones, and flesh of my flesh:

She shall be called Woman, because she was taken out of Man."

What Would You Say?

Verses 19 and 20 seem at first like a digression. Why do you think God had Adam name all of the animals before He made the Woman?

Man, God formed from mud, but woman, God made of living flesh. Thus man was the crown of creation, and woman the diamond in the crown. We must observe that human beings are not meant to live alone and that marriage is the normal state of human society. Marriage and family are not results of sin but are righteous and wholesome. Furthermore, a marriage is the beginning of a new family, as verse 24 points out. A man leaves his parents to become "one flesh" with his wife. The fact that the first woman was literally created from the flesh of man is to be continually reflected in the intimacy of the marriage bond, one so close that the two live as one.

Humanity As a Race

Before leaving our study of the nature of man, we must go beyond the makeup of individuals to the corporate nature of humanity. By this we mean that God created mankind as a race. God made the first couple, but afterward people make people. We are all related by literal family ties—one has merely to look far enough back in history.

We can divide our corporate nature into two aspects: family and society. To say it differently, we all have close relations with certain people and distant relations with many other people. Part of our human nature is our interrelationship with others.

Family—

First, we will face up to what God says about family. I say "face up" because this strikes us all where we know we fail. Have you ever thought about what God wants of your family? Or what He expects of you when you lead your own family someday?

God has entrusted parents with great power to affect their children. Sinful people often use this power for evil, but it can be used to accomplish even more good. As a child, you have borne either the burdens of poor parentage or the great blessings of godly parentage. You had no chance to choose which. As a parent, you will have power to do great good or great harm to your own children regardless of their desires. This is a tremendous responsibility God has given to man.

God did not make humans to live in isolation. Even for flawless Adam it was not good to be alone. Adam had God's fellowship, but God knew that Adam needed another of his own kind. But the second human would not be identical to the first one. God expresses His glory in variety—in fact, He doesn't seem to make any two things exactly alike. So the second human, a woman, was not a copy of Adam but a complement to him. A *complement* is a completer. Thus God established the foundational component of human society—the family.

Eden's model family provides a pattern to show us what a family is supposed to be. One man with one woman, bonded by love, for life. This family was complete without children. Likewise, you will not marry strictly for the purpose of having children.

However, children are part of the normal course of a family. Children are in both God's image and in their parents' image. We should prize children and treasure them in the same way God treasures us.

Any perversion of the family pattern will result in destruction, just as eating from Eden's forbidden fruit did. In other words, violating the family structure is *sin.* Sodomy and lesbianism, adultery (and all other extramarital sex), and divorce are sins against God that injure those who commit them along with everyone whose lives they touch. Divorce hurts the couple that divorces and their children with them. Adultery wounds at least three souls, often many more. Homosexuality cannot be an alternative pattern for the family, for it is sin, a wicked perversion expressly forbidden and condemned (Gen. 19; I Cor. 6:9).

However, the family is damaged even when any of the above sins is only in the heart of a family member. Although a husband may not actually divorce his wife, if he hates her, he is sinning before God and corroding his family. Likewise, avoiding actual adultery does not excuse a husband's pornography or a wife's lusting for other men. Sin of the heart is still sin.

Probably, some friends of yours or you personally have suffered because of these sins. Perhaps your parents are divorced; perhaps they are not divorced but act as if they would like to be. Perhaps you have engaged in extramarital sex or even homosexual acts. Such sins do not separate you from the love of God in Jesus Christ, but you must confess to God that you have sinned. Call those things *sins,* not mistakes or defeats. If you have no remorse for sins, you reveal that you may well have never been saved.

Let me make it clear that physical attraction to the opposite sex is not sin. On the contrary, it is part of God's wholesome design. But your natural desires and the thoughts they conjure must always be bound to the context of marriage. God's plan and the pattern He set from the beginning is for one man to marry one woman and for them to cleave faithfully to one another for life. That is God's plan and the pattern He established in the beginning. As such, it is also the pathway to the purest and richest joy.

Society—

Beyond our families, we are all members of a broader society. We belong to certain nations, and what *we* are makes up what our nations are. Nations are not abstract ideologies; they are living conglomerates of people with various values, morals, occupations, and desires. Christians are salt and light in the world (Matt. 5:13-16). God renders mercy and kindness to nations because His people dwell in them (Gen. 39:1-5; 41:41-57). Even as a minority, Christians have a tremendous potential to do good to the surrounding society through evangelism and discipleship, through public stands for righteousness, through social benevolence, and through unceasing intercessory prayer.

Conversely, societal sin affects us along with everyone else. It is not that society sins as a whole, but rather that when individuals sin they affect the whole society. Your nation pays a price when particular sins are encouraged or even tolerated. Wickedness in government brings a reproach on the country. Unjust wars, ethnic genocide, sanctioned murder (like infant abortion), and rampant sexual immorality invite God's wrath.

Notice that government should restrain some of these sins, such as murder. Others, like hatred and greed, are outside the domain of government and must be overcome by spiritual revival. Either way, God's people are responsible to promote godliness and resist wickedness in their societies.

God made the first man and woman, and they are the parents of us all. God entrusted them with power to set the course for the whole race. In the next section, we will see what happened when they chose evil instead of good.

Man Rebelled Against God

Now that we have looked at humanity as God created it, we want to study what happened when the first humans rebelled against God. This is the doctrine of sin. What exactly did man lose because of sin? How different is man from the way God originally created him?

You and all the people you interact with for your whole life are influenced by sin. Inside you are both the good creature God made and a sinner. It is necessary to learn and accept what God teaches us about sin in order to understand all human behavior. What is more, realizing the truth about sin is necessary to conquering it in your own life and in guiding others to do the same.

The Temptation and First Sin of Man

God created man (male and female) as perfect beings in a perfect environment, but He enabled them to serve Him voluntarily by giving them one way to disobey Him. With no way possible to disobey, they would have been virtual robots. They could not have chosen to obey God had there been no way to choose otherwise.

God established a single rule: the fruit of one particular tree in the Garden of Eden was off-limits (2:16-17). This test could

This sprawling graden in Versailles, France, gives some idea of what the Garden of Eden may have looked like.

hardly have been easier. First, it was a negative rule—don't do this. They weren't required to do something daily, which would be more demanding. Second, they had no compulsion to do this one thing because the Garden was full of fruit trees whose fruit they could eat. Do not think of the Garden as a vegetable patch. A river watered it, a river large enough to form four more rivers outside of Eden. The Garden had to have been a vast area, more than enough for two people.

However, God allowed one additional factor to complete the test. Without this factor, it may be that man never would have sinned. We must realize that, as the Lord made him, man had no nature to sin. It was the nature of humanity to do good. This means that every thought, impulse, and desire of the first humans' hearts was pure, loving, and righteous. God gave them a perfect nature like His own, but also gave them the power to choose to keep it or not. Under the influence of the one external factor, they chose to cast away their perfect nature.

That factor was a personal, intelligent being who appeared in the form of a serpent, or snake. Now we tend to think of snakes as bad, but that attitude is a consequence of the events in the Garden. Snakes were probably beautiful creatures. In any case, the woman had no reason to be suspicious of one. At that time all creatures were harmless and under her dominion.

In Genesis 3 the serpent is said to be more crafty, or devious, than any other animal. It addresses the woman. (On this point it is important not to be sidetracked by the fact that an animal could speak. Read Numbers 22 for a case of another talking animal.) But the snake was not speaking for itself. Comparison to later Scripture makes it apparent that this snake was Satan, the spiritual being who leads opposition to God and regularly tries to get people to sin. (See Job 1-2, Zechariah 3:1-2, and Revelation 12:9.)

Temptation

We must see several things in Genesis 3 about temptation and sin. The pattern the serpent uses to persuade the woman to disobey God appears throughout Scripture. The same sort of temptation draws us into sin today. We have to recognize Satan's strategy of temptation and know how to defeat it.

First, the serpent casts doubt on the character of God by focusing the woman's attention on the one rule. He implies that God's restriction is unjust because there is no reason for it. Second, he directly denies God's Word (v. 4). Third, he accuses God of jealousy and selfishness. Fourth, in the same breath, he appeals to the woman's natural (and righteous) desire to be like God as a reason to rebel against God!

Verse 6 says that the woman concluded three things about the fruit of the forbidden tree: it was good for food, it had a pleasing appearance, and it would bring the eater to unknown wisdom. On these bases, she eats it. Then she gives it to Adam, and he eats it, presumably for the same reasons. Thus, man sinned; the serpent deceived the woman, the woman disobeyed God, and then the woman gave the fruit to the man and he disobeyed God too.

TEMPTATIONS

	GEN. 3	LUKE 4 (MATT 4)	I JOHN 2:16
Physical Needs	good for food	stones to bread	lust of the flesh
Possessions	delight to the eyes	kingdoms of earth	lust of the eyes
Experience	fruit to make wise	jump from the pinnacle	pride of life

We have to make some key observations about temptation before moving on to the result of temptation, sin. The first is that temptation appeals to you to fulfill legitimate God-given desires in ways that God has forbidden. God had given man fruit in order to eat and live, beautiful things to possess and enjoy, and the power to learn and master the world. Every time they did these things they became a little more like God. They were made in God's image, so God-*likeness* was not itself an evil goal.

Since the woman was a good being without evil thoughts, possibly the serpent convinced her that eating the fruit was what God actually wanted her to do. Perhaps its first question, "Has God really said . . . ?" cast doubt on her own understanding of God's prohibition. But the prohibition had been clear, and the woman's mistake was in breaking the specific command of God.

The second observation is that the same three appeals still tempt humans to sin. First John 2:16 defines worldly wickedness as the lust of the flesh, the lust of the eyes, and the pride of life. These three are parallel to the serpent's three temptations. Humans still sin out of their desire for life (gluttony), their desire for possessions (covetousness), and their desire to experience and know more than others (pride).

Sin

Finally we come to the reality of sin itself. There are several very important facts about sin that every Christian must clearly understand. Sin is a major topic in the Bible. God is not cruel for teaching us about sin; on the contrary, He loves us by showing us how severely wicked we are.

Misconceptions about sin can cause overreliance on human efforts and even false presentations of the gospel, which can in turn lead people to think they are saved when they are not. Sin cannot be cured merely by confession or penitence ("making up for" a sin some way) or by behavior seminars. Sin is not a social disease, nor is it due to your background (although others' sin can worsen your own sin). A seemingly good person may well be a doomed sinner before God.

Think About It! One of the ever-present problems in Christian theology is the existence of evil. Evil first appears in the serpent in the Garden. The problem is mainly logical and philosophical because the Bible never explicitly explains where Satan came from. But the quandary is this: if God is all-powerful and all-knowing, why didn't He dispose of Satan from the beginning—or, better yet, never even create him? There is ultimately no answer to this question in Scripture. We know only that God creates beings with the responsibility to choose right. Some choose evil, but no sin goes unpunished or defeats God's purposes.

First, exactly what was the woman's sin? We must say that it was not a lie, as it may appear in verse 3. She could not have lied because lying about God's Word would have been the first sin, not eating forbidden fruit. The fact is that only one way to sin was available to the woman. Apparently God had truly told the humans not to touch the tree of knowledge of good and evil.

Second, why did the serpent tempt the woman instead of the man? We are not told. The man may have been elsewhere, but nothing in the text indicates this. He was evidently standing there listening to the conversation. It may be that the woman was more trusting or that the woman swayed the man more easily than the serpent could have persuaded him directly.

All of these possibilities are speculative. What we must emphasize is that they both ate before they both were ashamed. The image is that the woman made her choice, picked one fruit with each hand, bit one while handing her husband the other one. Although the effects were slightly different upon the man and woman, the point is that man sinned, male and female, plunging themselves and their descendants into sin.

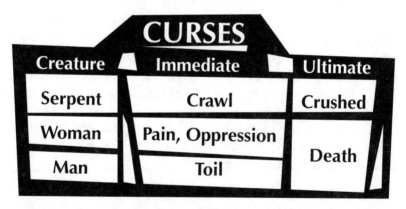

CURSES		
Creature	**Immediate**	**Ultimate**
Serpent	**Crawl**	**Crushed**
Woman	**Pain, Oppression**	**Death**
Man	**Toil**	

Next, what are the consequences of sin? The first parents were immediately conscious of their nakedness, signifying their guilt before God. The very nature of human beings changed from good and pure to evil and corrupt. Instead of joyful communion with God, there is shame and fear. When challenged, they each shift blame for their sin to another: the man blames the woman and the woman blames the serpent (Gen. 3:8-13).

This incident is what theologians call the Fall of man, meaning his fall from the perfect state in which he was created into his present state of sinful defilement and rebellion against God. What immediately followed is called the Curse (3:14-19). First the serpent is cursed directly, then the woman and the man receive consequences for their sins.

Women experience great pain in childbirth. The pain appears to have dual significance: the child is born a sinner due (partly) to the first mother's sin; second, the seed of the woman (a child born to a woman, namely Jesus Christ) would eventually overcome sin and its damage by defeating the serpent.

The man's sin resulted in a curse on the earth. Men have to work hard in order to eat. Man was always supposed to work, but it was not to be laborious or painful.

However, the main consequence of the fall is *death*. As God had warned, Adam and Eve effectively died when they sinned, for they were dead to God. Furthermore, the decay began that eventually put them back into the ground.

Original Sin

Romans explains clearly what Genesis relates with a story—humanity became sinful by nature when Adam sinned. God gave Adam the power to propagate a race of his own kind and to impart his nature to them. Had Adam imparted his perfect, righteous nature, it would have been the greatest gift he could give. But his sin cost not only him but also all his descendants their righteousness.

All human beings commit sins because they are sinners. Our thoughts and impulses lead instinctively to sin, not goodness. This is not to say that all of us are as bad as we can be or that sinners cannot do good things. But Scripture says that even the righteous acts of people are worthless before Him.

We pause to ask, was God unjust to let the whole race fall because of one man's sin? In response, remember that Adam was no ordinary man. He was the father of all mankind, and he was created perfectly sinless. He had everything going for him, as it were. Moreover, the power God entrusted to him could even more easily have been used for good, and the good would have would have been far greater than the evil that resulted instead. Therefore, Adam bears much of the blame for the sin of mankind.

GOD IS RIGHTEOUS

1. Adam could have chosen right and blessed us all.
2. Every human commits his own sins.
3. God has provided salvation for everyone who wants it.

Furthermore, every human commits actual sins, so God is not unjust to punish us. It would contradict His very nature to allow sin and not punish it. And our sin is our fault, not His. He doesn't actually punish anyone for Adam's sin. We all die because of our own sins.

Finally, God is just because He made provision for the salvation of every human being who wants salvation more than he wants sin. Of course, God would have been just even if He had not made a way of salvation, but His self-sacrificing provision for our salvation proves how unassailably fair He is. God took it on Himself to replace the failed obedience of Adam with the obedience of Christ Jesus who became the new head of the new human race, the saved believers in Christ.

Nature of Sin

Before finishing, we must examine what the Bible teaches about sin itself. It is helpful to study the particular words used for sin in the Bible. There is not so general a word as the English word *sin* in either Hebrew or Greek, the main languages of the Bible. They have collections of words used to describe sin.

DID YOU KNOW? Adam is called the "Federal Head" of the human race because his sin caused the fall of the race. *Federal* refers to an organization in which a central authority rules over lesser authorities and acts as their representative in matters that affect the whole. For example, the United States has a federal government that rules over the individual state governments and represents them to the rest of the world.

Hebrew and Greek use words like rebellion, transgression, failure, pollution, and stubbornness. **Rebellion** is actively violating known law in direct conflict with the authority that made the law and attempting to overthrow that authority. **Transgression** is going out of bounds and doing something that is forbidden. **Pollution** is rot—like disease or mold that corrupts everything it touches. **Stubbornness** is steady refusal to repent when rebuked, so that even when the knowledge of God is presented people refuse to respond as they should.

What Would You Say?

What if the first parents had rebuffed the serpent and obeyed God? We cannot know for sure, but it seems that such a victory would have led to the very prize the serpent persuaded them to seek illegitimately. They would have gained the knowledge of good and evil by choosing good instead of evil. But it would have been like the knowledge of God who knows evil without experiencing it and thus remains perfectly holy. Perhaps we never would have sinned if our parents had passed this one test. This question is in an area beyond our understanding, but it is important to realize the damage a single sin can do.

Ezekiel 1–3 shows us that sin is not merely inadequacy but active rebellion. People are stubborn, hard-faced, and stiff-necked. People don't sin because they are ignorant of God, but because they hate Him and everything He values.

The Bible's description of humanity graphically illustrates man's position of hostility to God:

The wicked are estranged from the womb: they go astray as soon as they be born, speaking lies (Ps. 58:3).

They are corrupt, they have done abominable works, there is none that doeth good. The Lord looked down from heaven upon the children of men, to see if there were any that did understand, and seek God. They are all gone aside, they are all together become filthy: there is none that doeth good, no, not one (Ps. 14:1-3).

But we are all as an unclean thing, and all our righteousnesses are as filthy rags (Isa. 64:6).

What is man, that he should be clean? and he which is born of a woman, that he should be righteous? Behold, [God] putteth no trust in his saints; yea, the heavens are not clean in his sight. How much more abominable and filthy is man, which drinketh iniquity like water (Job 15:14-16)?

Judgment on Sin

God made you with a sense of justice. You and I know instinctively that wrong should be punished and restitution made for any injuries. It's a moral necessity. The questions are What is wrong? and How does one know the right punishment or restitution?

Suppose you are a judge with absolute power. Think through what you would do in the following situation: a young man is brought before you who has murdered one of his own friends. The evidence is solid, and he doesn't even deny the crime. He planned the murder in advance and was not in any way threatened by his victim.

What is his punishment? Answering that question reveals much about your sense of justice. If you think he should immediately be executed, it shows that you have a serious sense of justice. If you decide he should somehow make restitution or spend the rest of his life in prison, it shows you take crime seriously but not with the same philosophy of punishment. If you want to know more of his personal situation—his motive, his remorsefulness—before deciding his penalty, it shows that you believe that more than simple facts matter in justice.

This scenario is not a matter of right and wrong decisions, it is a way to illustrate the decisions a judge must make. On what basis does a judge rule? He rules on the basis of his belief about justice.

God is the judge of all mankind by right of creation and moral supremacy. He judges based on what He considers right, not what you or I or anyone else considers right. Just as the defendant's refusal to admit he deserves punishment does not force the judge to acquit him, so my ideas of justice do not compel God to deal with me in a certain way. He deals with me in the way He Himself determines, for He has both the absolute moral right and the power to do as He wishes.

God judges sin. God punishes sinners. The Bible says that His judgment is both on earth and in eternity. His judgments vary in degrees and over time, but His ultimate punishment for sin is eternal suffering in the lake of fire (Matt. 25:41; Rev. 20:14-15).

Is this shocking or disturbing? It should be. Is it impossible to reconcile the doctrine of a just, loving, and merciful God with the doctrine of eternal punishment? The problem lies in our failure to understand the severity of sin. According to God's sense of justice (which is absolutely right because God Himself is the measure of right and wrong), even one sin demands absolute punishment.

Conclusion

God made man upright, but man sinned and shattered his own righteousness. The good and pure condition in which the first man and woman existed was lost. The image of God was marred, and man became sinful by nature. In the scope of Scripture as a whole, the sin of man is significant because it shows the need for a Savior. Therefore, the next two chapters in this book deal with Jesus Christ and the way of salvation.

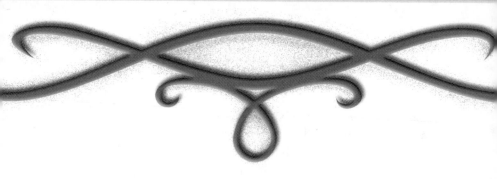

Come, Ye Sinners

Joseph Hart, 1712-1768

Come, ye sinners, poor and needy,
Weak and wounded, sick and sore;
Jesus ready stands to save you,
Full of pity, love, and power;
He is able, He is able,
He is willing; doubt no more.

Now, ye needy, come and welcome;
God's free bounty glorify;
True belief and true repentance,
Every grace that brings you nigh;
Without money, Without money,
Come to Jesus Christ and buy.

Come, ye weary, heavy laden,
Bruised and mangled by the fall;
If you tarry till you're better,
You will never come at all;
Not the righteous, Not the righteous;
Sinners Jesus came to call.

CHAPTER FOUR

The Word of Life

4

Memory Verses: John 1:1-5, 14

---

1. Which of these men was essential to Buddhism?   **D**
   a. Siddhartha Gautama   b. Upali   c. Ananda   d. none of the above
2. Which of these men was essential to Islam?   **D**
   a. Muhammad   b. Avicenna   c. Averroes   d. none of the above
3. Which of these men was essential to Christianity?   **A**
   a. Jesus Christ   b. Paul   c. Augustine   d. none of the above

---

Could Buddhism exist if Gautama Buddha had never lived? The answer is yes; Buddhism could be just as it is even if someone else had first "reached Enlightenment."

Could Islam exist if the prophet Muhammad had never lived? The answer is yes. According to its own doctrine, Islam could be the same even if Allah had chosen some other man to be his latest prophet.

Could Christianity exist if Jesus Christ had never lived? The answer is no. According to the New Testament, Christ is the very heart of Christianity. No other man, or other being of any kind, could have replaced Him. Christ Himself is the unique instrument whose perfect righteousness, undeserved death, and resurrection to life are indispensable to the salvation of human beings. Only Christ was both fully human and fully God. There could be no second such "God-man" at any time in history. If the biblical Christian faith is true, it excludes all other religions. Biblical Christianity rests on the person and work of Jesus Christ.

GET THE BIG
PICTURE

   I. The Person of Jesus Christ
      A. Person and Nature
      B. The Virgin Birth of Christ
      C. Christ in the Old Testament
   II. The Work of Christ
      A. Christ's Offices
      B. Stages in Christ's Work

The previous chapter examined the Bible's teaching about the human race. Scripture records how man came into being, what God meant man to be, and how the first man and woman failed to obey God when tested. Now we want to study the next logical part of theology—what God did on account of man's failure.

This chapter will survey what the Bible says about the person and work of the Lord Jesus Christ. This subject is called **Christology,** from *Christos* and *logos,* meaning the study of Christ. Christ's person is who He is, and Christ's work is what He did (and does). The Bible itself acknowledges this two-part division in Matthew 16:21. When the disciples understood that Christ was God, they were ready to learn of His mission.

The Person of Jesus Christ

Exactly who was Jesus Christ? Virtually no one denies that He was a historical person who lived during the first years of the era named in His honor, between 5 B.C. and A.D. 35 (see box). However, the Bible records both His own claims and abundant testimony that He is more than an ordinary man. He is God.

Let's first consider two basic errors people make about the Lord Jesus. These errors have several varieties, but they can be thought of simply as opposite extremes. The first error is to consider Christ a man who was not entirely God. The second error is

Calendar Question

B.C. stands for "before Christ," and A.D. is an abbreviation for *anno Domini,* a Latin phrase meaning "in the year of the Lord." This calendar system was not invented until centuries after Christ's earthly ministry, and it appears to modern scholarship that the calendar's inventor miscalculated the date of Christ's birth by a few years. Hence, Christ may have been born as early as 5 B.C., even though that means "five years before Christ."

to consider Christ God but not fully human. Both errors are equally destructive to the person and work of Christ.

Christological Controversies

In the early years of the Church, controversies erupted over some of the most basic doctrines. All of the apostles had died, leaving Christians responsible to interpret and obey the completed Bible without their guidance. Naturally, it took some time for prayerful study and reflection to define what the Bible taught.

Most significant of early controversies were those concerning the person of Christ. The Trinity had been debated and settled earlier. It followed that, once Christ was asserted to be part of the Trinity, more questions would arise about His person. Since Christ is essential to Christianity, defining Christ's person is essential to Christianity.

The controversies followed a similar course. Christians in one area would start teaching something about Christ to correct what they saw as an error. Other Christians would counter their arguments. Sometimes it was a question of heresy; sometimes it was just a difference of emphasis. Some controversies raged for decades and even centuries.

Remember two lessons from those early controversies whenever you are embroiled in an argument among Christians (or anyone, for that matter): first, emotions and politics run ahead of reason; second, people who resist an error tend to overreact, entering an opposite error. Stay level-headed, be patient, and collect all the facts. Wise decisions take time to formulate.

Huge gatherings of Christian ministers, called Church councils, met to settle these disputes. The "Christological Councils" arrived at what has been regarded ever since as the correct biblical doctrine of Christ. In other words, virtually anyone who calls himself "Christian" would agree with what the councils decided.

There were four major controversies. The table below lists each controversy. (The names come from the men who originated the arguments; for example, Nestorianism was begun by Nestorius.)

Controversies over the Person of Christ

NAME	ERROR	BIBLE DOCTRINES
Arianism	Christ is only human.	Christ is fully God.
Apollinarianism	Christ is only God.	Christ is fully human.
Nestorianism	Christ is two persons.	Christ is only one Person.
Eutychianism	Christ has only one nature.	Christ has two distinct natures.

Commonly you will hear that Jesus Christ was a good man and a wise teacher, but that of course He was not God. However well-intentioned, this position is logically impossible. Since He claimed to be deity, promised eternal life, forgave sins, and condemned unbelievers, He could hardly have been a good man if He were not God. If Jesus was not deity, He was either a liar who deliberately misled people or a self-deluded fool. As we will see, Scripture claims that Jesus was deity.

On the other hand, you may encounter the more subtle error that Jesus Christ was supernatural (divinity, if not deity) but was not entirely human. This is a heresy that goes almost as far back as the former error. First-century false teachers asserted that the Christ (a deity) descended on a mortal man (Jesus of Nazareth) and departed from him shortly before he was crucified.

Be aware of similar errors in different guises today. Many cults hold one or the other error about the Lord Jesus. However, one doesn't have to be a cultist to mistakenly emphasize one aspect of Christ's Person at the expense of the other. This is a danger for every Christian. Even in our own minds we can think of Christ as God and forget that, as a man, He fully sympathizes with our weaknesses (Heb. 4:15). Conversely, we can think of Jesus as a wonderful man but forget that He wields all the fearsome holiness and power of God (Rev. 1:12-20).

You learned in your study of the Trinity that Christ is God even though there is only one God and that Christ is distinct from God the Father. This is a paradox, a situation in which two or more propositions do not actually contradict each other but do not logically reconcile. That is, the logical implications of the propositions do contradict, but the Bible doesn't actually state those implications.

To be specific, the logical implication of the first and second propositions, "Christ is God" and "There is only one God," is that Christ *alone* is God. However, the Bible also teaches that Christ is distinct from God the Father. The implication may be strictly logical, but it is not biblical. The Bible never states the logical implications that would follow any two of the three propositions. For example, it never says "Christ alone is God" or "There are two Gods: Jesus and the Father." These implications are not true because they contradict whichever proposition they were not founded upon.

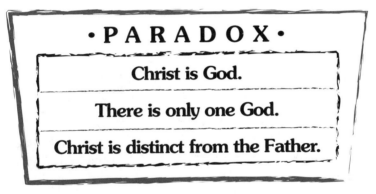

· P A R A D O X ·

Christ is God.

There is only one God.

Christ is distinct from the Father.

The Bible is never illogical, and normally the logical implications of a scriptural statement can be trusted as truth. But in a few instances, the spiritual reality behind what the Bible reveals is beyond the power of humans to comprehend. The Bible never addresses these paradoxes directly. It speaks in the plainest terms possible without being inaccurate.

How can you know when to trust logical conclusions from Scripture? Suspect them only when they contradict another clear statement of Scripture. But even then, withhold your judgment and continue studying. You may come across something that clears up the apparent contradiction. There are only a handful of paradoxes in Scripture; they all concern the most sophisticated

Complementary Terms

Person: An independent being with individual
intellect and conscience

Nature: The essence of a thing that makes it what it is

problems in human-divine interaction, and different Christians have scrutinized them for centuries.

With all of this in mind you will not be surprised by the difficulty of putting in systematic terms exactly who and what the Lord Jesus is. Taking all the Scriptures together, we see that Christ is one Person who has two natures. To understand this description we must define *person* and *nature* and the relationship between the two.

Person and Nature

A *person* is an independent being with individual intellect and conscience. Christ is not two separate persons, one human and

> **• TWO ERRORS •**
>
> **Christ is a man but not fully God.**
>
> **Christ is God but not fully human.**

one God. He is one person just as you are one person. You remember that the Trinity is the three persons of God: the Father, Son, and Holy Spirit. Christ is the second person of those three, God the Son.

Something's *nature* is the essence of that thing that makes it what it is. This is obviously not a scientific definition, but it is an important concept. To illustrate, think of trees. There are different types of trees and many different trees of each type, but each one has the nature of a tree. They look like trees, grow like trees,

reproduce like trees, and so forth. A tree, of course, does not have the nature of a flower or of a goose or of a killer whale.

This may be painfully obvious, but it helps our minds to recognize the level of wonder that Jesus Christ has two natures. Nothing should have two natures (by definition), but Christ does. He has the nature of God as well as the nature of a man.

Now we have to consider the relationship between two natures in one person. Does the Bible suggest that Christ sometimes acts according to His human nature and other times acts according to His divine nature? Do His two natures conflict with each other so that Christ constantly has to deal with some kind of psycho-spiritual schizophrenia?

In Scripture we see the Lord always acting with a single purpose. With the exception of one passage (see box), there is no indication of any struggle between Christ as man and Christ as God. Consider how this makes sense when you think of the previous chapter on the study of man. Christ was sinless as a man— His humanity was of the perfect order in which God created Adam and Eve. Just as they were in perfect harmonious fellowship with God, so Christ's perfect human nature was completely compatible with His "God-ness."

Christ's Two Wills

The only point in Christ's earthly ministry at which a possible conflict between His two natures appears is in Luke 22:39-44, the agony in the Garden of Gethsemane. In verse 42, the Lord prays to God the Father, "not my will, but Thine, be done." He seems to indicate that His will differed from the Father's. Perhaps Christ's human nature shrank from the suffering of the Cross. Perhaps He was referring to the agony He was undergoing in the garden, and verse 23 was an answer from the Father. In any case, Jesus submitted to the Father's will as a perfect human always does.

One of the great conflicts in the early Church arose over the question of Christ's two wills. It isn't nearly as important as the other early conflicts: Christ's deity, humanity, and origin. But it was a big deal at the time, and the "orthodox" position was that Christ does indeed have a human will distinct from His divine will on the basis of Luke 22:42.

We should all take great comfort in the fact that Christ is living proof that man and God can be in unbroken fellowship. While sin taints us now, keeping us out of immediate communion with our Lord, when it is completely gone, fellowship will be fully restored. Even during life, there is no ultimate limit to the level of joyful friendship you can have with the Lord. Only sin hinders you. As the Holy Spirit progressively frees you from sin and changes you into the righteous image of Jesus Christ, the relationship God intends for people to have with Himself increasingly becomes your own.

Christ's two natures are inseparable yet unmixed. He will never cease to be God, and He will never cease to be man. But He is not some hybrid creature who is a blend of God and humanity without being fully either. There is a free communication of properties by the two.

The Lord's dual nature appears in several ways in the gospels. He claimed to be a man (John 8:40) and He claimed to be equal with God (John 10:30-38). He grew tired and hungry (John 4:6; Matt. 21:18) but worked miracles, including the creation of food and drink (John 2:1-11; Matt. 14:13-21). The transfiguration was a powerful visible manifestation of His normally hidden divine glory (Matt. 17:1-9).

Perhaps the clearest case is the Lord's use of His omniscience during His earthly ministry. At times He displayed supernatural knowledge (John 1:48) and at other times the normal human limitation of knowledge (John 11:34). Christ knew what He needed to know to advance His ministry and demonstrate His identity as Son of God. He did not display omniscience when it was not necessary, when simply asking questions got Him the information He needed. In this way the Lord Jesus demonstrated that He was both humanity and deity.

Think About It!

The Hebrew word for "virgin" is a common word for a young woman. It does not necessarily emphasize virginity as the English word *virgin* does. This fact leads some people to deny that Isaiah 7:14 prophesies the virgin birth of Christ. But Isaiah declares that the birth would be a "sign," a miraculous display of God's power. Nothing is special about some unknown young woman bearing a child. Furthermore, the Hebrew word normally implies virginity, much like the older English word *maiden*. Finally, the Greek version of the Old Testament uses a word that does specifically mean virgin.

The Virgin Birth of Christ

Previous Old Testament prophecies of the Messiah had revealed that He would be both man and God, but only Isaiah 7:14 prophesies that He would be born of a virgin. In that chapter, faithless King Ahaz of Israel refused to ask for a miraculous sign from God because he had no intention of trusting God to save his kingdom from enemy attack. God responds through Isaiah the prophet that He will give a "sign" of His own choosing. It will be the birth of a special child born to a virgin.

Early in the twentieth century a major controversy arose over the virgin birth of Christ. Belief in the virgin birth became one key test of whether or not someone believed the Bible. The reason was that, in those years, unbelievers were largely naturalistic or anti-supernatural. In other words, they had a supposedly scientific mindset that ruled out anything miraculous.

In your lifetime, you may encounter unbelievers of a very different type who believe in the supernatural—even in miracles— but reject the full deity of Jesus Christ. We say *full* deity because some agree Jesus was divine, but deny that He was God Himself. They think He was a man who achieved divinity and that other people, even you or I, could potentially do the same. You have to be prepared to answer critics of either kind, those who disbelieve the supernatural and those who believe in it so readily that they cheapen miracles and make them commonplace.

Of course, even without the prophecy in Isaiah there is no room for a Bible believer to deny the doctrine of the virgin birth of Christ. The apostle Luke under the Holy Spirit's inspiration wrote explicitly that the mother of the Lord was a virgin. On this basis we can be sure that God intended to foretell a miraculous virgin birth for the Messiah in Isaiah 7:14.

Christ in the Old Testament

The person and work of Jesus Christ is the central theme of the Bible. We can trace the revelation of Christ from Genesis 3 forward. In this section we will examine a series of the most important Old Testament passages concerning Christ.

Every Christian must realize that the Old Testament is as much the revelation of Jesus Christ as the New Testament is. You must continually read and digest the entire Bible to grow as a Christian. The key for you personally to unlock what the Old Testament means is to understand its ultimate connection to the Lord Jesus.

Christological Prophesies in Genesis		
3:15	Human	Savior from Sin
9:27	Shem's Descendant	Deity
12:3	Abraham's Descendant	Worldwide Blessing
49:10	Judah's Descendant	Israel's Ruler

We looked at the creation and fall of man in the last chapter. Immediately after the first human sin, God decreed that the seed of the woman would crush the serpent's head, though the serpent would strike the seed's own heel (Gen. 3:15). Thus from the very beginning of Scripture we expect a human being to undo the damage done by the serpent but to suffer for it in some way.

Noah added the next prophecy of this special man (Gen. 9:27). The Lord, Noah says, will enlarge Japheth (from whom are descended the majority of people on earth) but dwell in the tents of Shem. This brief reference reveals that the special man would be God Himself and that He would come from Shem's descent.

God's promise to Abraham expressed that through Abraham's line would come a worldwide blessing (Gen. 12:3). Abraham's descendants received a particular land as their own. The right to rule over the chosen nation went to Judah (Gen. 49:10) until "Shiloh" came, a word that means "he whose it is"; that is, the real owner of the kingship delegated to Judah.

All these points in the first book of the Bible show us that the Anointed One would be human, would be God, would be Abraham's descendant, would bless the whole human race, and would be Judah's descendant with the right to rule Israel.

Later in the Old Testament, when the descendants of Israel were a nation, their kings prefigured Christ. Second Samuel 7 forecasts Christ, the perpetual king, with God's promise that the throne of David would be established forever (v. 16). Every king of Israel and Judah, by fact of his office, was a picture of Christ. Both of the Lord's human parents were descendants of King David, whose kingship Christ now occupies (Acts 2:30).

The Book of Psalms contains many prophecies of Jesus Christ. Psalm 2 records God's declaration to His Son that the Son would be king of Zion (Jerusalem) and king over all the kings of the earth. Also, everyone who trusts that Son will be blessed.

The Work of Christ

Now that we have considered who Christ is, we have to examine what Christ did for your sake and mine. We call this the work of Christ. There are important aspects of Christ's work that are ongoing (things He is still doing today). Other aspects Christ has finished, such as His earthly life, death, and resurrection. The ongoing works are extensions of His finished work in the way that farming is the continual work of a farmer who first built his farm.

Christ's Offices

Theologians often classify Christ's work according to His three offices: priest, king, and prophet. We might also call them functions or roles. Each of His offices is mirrored by God's people in the Old Testament. Israel's priests, kings, and prophets served the dual purpose of revealing part of the truth about

Messiah while at the same time demonstrating the ultimate inadequacy of humans to fulfill His offices. The Pentateuch (Genesis-Deuteronomy) shows the need for a perfect priest who can offer a perfect sacrifice. The history books (Joshua-Chronicles) show the need for a perfect king who will not sin. The prophetic books (Isaiah-Malachi) show the need for a perfect prophet to reveal God.

• T H R E E   O F F I C E S •

Priest • King • Prophet

Priest

In the Old Testament, Israel's Levitical priesthood was mainly concerned with sacrifices. Think about the English word *sacrifices* for a moment. It covers a group of Hebrew words for the individual offerings that share a common element: worshipers gave up something valuable in order to serve the Lord. Although some sacrifices consisted of grain or wine, most were animals. These were blood sacrifices, living creatures killed to fulfill the purposes of God.

What were God's purposes in having innocent animals killed? To answer this question we must neither overvalue nor undervalue animal life. Animals are not in God's image; they have no moral sense and do neither righteousness nor evil. Killing an animal is not murder. However, they are of greater "value" than plants, for as flesh-and-blood creatures with consciousness and sensitivity they are similar to human life.

Death is the necessary punishment for sin. Animal death, then, tangibly pictures the result of sin. Animals don't sin, yet people had to carry out the killing of sacrificial animals.

God's purposes in the Old Testament sacrifices were manifold, but they all amounted to object lessons on the work of Jesus Christ (Col. 2:17; Heb. 10:1). Jesus committed no sin, but He bore the punishment for sin. Although Jesus' blood was shed by the hands of sinful men, His blood could cover the sins of those same men. Jesus truly belonged to God, but it was God's will that He die for the sake of sinners.

Israel's high priest offered the most important sacrifice of the year, the sacrifice on the Day of Atonement. On this day, the high priest took the slain lamb's blood inside the innermost sanctum of the Tabernacle (later the Temple) and sprinkled it on the "mercy seat," which was the top of the ark of the Covenant. Within the ark of the covenant were the two tablets of the Law that God gave Moses. The symbolism was that, though the people could not keep the Law of God, the shed blood "covered" the Law in the people's behalf.

As the New Testament book of Hebrews says, this system had a great flaw: it had to be repeated every year (Heb. 9:7). The author's conclusion is that it really accomplished nothing. It only prophesied the priestly work of Christ, the perfect priest, who would offer Himself, the perfect sacrifice, to make atonement for all sins once and forever (Heb. 9:25-28). Thus, we say that the work of Christ as priest was to atone for the sin of mankind and to reconcile God and man through His sacrifice.

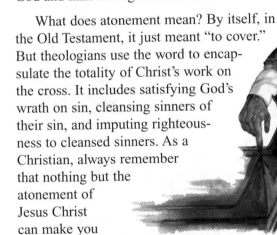

What does atonement mean? By itself, in the Old Testament, it just meant "to cover." But theologians use the word to encapsulate the totality of Christ's work on the cross. It includes satisfying God's wrath on sin, cleansing sinners of their sin, and imputing righteousness to cleansed sinners. As a Christian, always remember that nothing but the atonement of Jesus Christ can make you righteous before God.

A classic disagreement in the history of Christian theology is the extent of the atonement. The problem is this: the atonement of Christ extends to the whole world (I John 2:2), but many people will never be saved (Rev. 20). How is it possible for Christ to die in the place of sinners who never trust Him for salvation? If Christ took the punishment for their sins, how can they still undergo that punishment?

The problem is more of a logical quandary than a scriptural one, but all Christians should be aware of it. There are three ways to a solution. First, we can say that Christ did not die for the sins of those who die unsaved. Second, we can say that Christ died for everyone's sins, but God's wrath remains upon unbelievers. Third, we might establish a balanced position trying to affirm exactly as much as the Bible affirms.

The third position is preferable, but even it has variants. Christians differ on the details of the solution. One traditional explanation is that Christ's atonement was sufficient for all, but efficient only for people who trust Christ. In other words, Christ's blood had unlimited potential to atone for sins, but it actually cleansed only those who had been or would be saved.

If none of the answers quite satisfies you, don't worry. It would not be a problem if it had an easy answer.

King

Scripture leaves no doubt that Jesus Christ is the ruler of the world. He rules both by right of inheritance (Col. 1:15; John 18:36-37) and by right of merit (Rev. 5:9-13). He is king already (John 18:37; Rev. 1:5), but His rule will be personal and direct when He returns to earth (Jer. 23:5; Rev. 17:14).

Living in a modern republic, you may find it hard to imagine just how powerful a true king really is. He is the principal lawmaker, chief executive, and highest judge. He decides policy on both domestic and international affairs. He governs the economy by setting taxes at will and writing the budget himself. He commands all armed forces and uses them to maintain control of his kingdom and to wage war against his enemies.

Similarly, Christ is the real governor of the world. Presently, He is our general who orchestrates all Christians in the execution of His divine plan. He actively protects us from evil and the attacks of the Devil and sinful people. In the future, He will come back to earth as king and establish direct rule, subduing all His enemies and enforcing righteousness. He will be king forever.

Prophet

A prophet is a spokesman for God. There are many prophets in the Old Testament. Anyone who conveys God's message to mankind is effectively a prophet, but those who received and passed on direct revelation are especially called prophets. The special class of prophets began with Samuel and continued through Malachi. Despite all of the prophets' faithful efforts, people remained obstinately sinful. The prophets helped to show the need for a perfect, or complete, revelation of God through a perfect prophet.

The Lord Jesus Christ is a prophet because He reveals the will of God to us. He is more than an ordinary human prophet because He is God. Human prophets in the Bible fell short, not because their prophecies contained mistakes, but because they could only relay what God had told them. As God in human flesh, Christ was God speaking directly to the human race. Moreover, Christ showed by His earthly life what Almighty God is like. His character, actions, and emotions as well as His words reveal God (Heb. 1:3). Thus, the Lord Jesus is the perfect prophet.

During His earthly ministry, Christ's primary message to man was "the gospel of the kingdom of God" (Mark 1:14). He thus revealed what He was about to do to complete salvation for human beings. We can say that, in revealing His own person and work, Christ showed us God the Father.

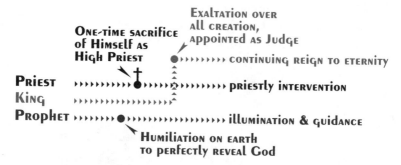

The Lord Jesus performed His latest act as a prophet when He delivered the Book of Revelation to John (Rev. 1:1). In that book Christ reveals the course of the end of human history and the setting up of the eternal kingdom in which He will reign forever.

Christ continues His revelatory work by teaching us the will of God through the ministry of the Holy Spirit (John 16:5-11). The Spirit guides our understanding of the Word of God and its application to us specifically.

Stages in Christ's Work

Mentally understanding what Christ *did* for our salvation and *does* for our ongoing sanctification is a major part of being a Christian. Understanding isn't enough by itself, of course; we have to respond to what we know. But knowing what He does is the necessary foundation to doing what He wants.

In the next chapter you will survey the way God brought about salvation itself. The last section of this chapter will prepare you for that by examining the work of Christ according to its two major stages: humiliation and exaltation.

Humiliation

Christ lived in eternity past with the Father and Holy Spirit in Heaven (John 1:1; Col. 1:17). Though He apparently came to earth periodically in the appearance of a man (Gen. 18), He did not actually take on human nature until conceived by the Holy Spirit in the womb of Mary. We call this descent from His position as God the Son in Heaven to earth as a mortal man the **humiliation** of Christ.

The word *humiliation* causes some difficulties. It tends to make us think of someone who is prideful getting what he deserves, or someone getting undeservedly embarrassed. Neither meaning is applicable to the humiliation of Christ. He was not proud, and He was not embarrassed. He humbled Himself by voluntarily giving up His exalted place in Heaven, where He received the praise and adulation He deserves, and taking on the limited, frail, inglorious body of a human being.

> **TERMS:**
> - **Humiliation**
>   - **-Active Obedience**
>   - **-Passive Obedience**
> - **Exaltation**

The details of the earthly life of the Lord magnify the depth of His humiliation. Even becoming a great human king, in a palace, surrounded by thousands of servants, would have been an extraordinary demotion for Jesus Christ. But He stooped much lower than that for us.

Jesus was born to a very poor family in a race subject to foreign domination. He submitted to the care and headship of mortal human parents. He became a carpenter, a simple common tradesman. As a carpenter, He worked with His hands for a living— enduring the same penalty for sin Adam earned for the whole human race. He had younger brothers and sisters that He probably had to take care of, since His human father, Joseph, is not mentioned again after Jesus was twelve years old.

Even during His public ministry, the Lord Jesus was lowly and subservient to the people who by rights should have served Him. He traveled around preaching without permanent shelter. He kept company with fishermen, whose feet He once washed, taking the role of a slave to men who were of low social class. In all this, God the Son lowered Himself as low as He could, offering proof that He can identify with any human being.

Remember that Jesus did not surrender the least bit of His power or righteousness or infinity. Rather, He temporarily gave up His glory. He identified with us, with what it is to be human. He endured the same weaknesses, temptations, and other limitations of humanity.

Why was this necessary? Because it enabled Him to earn righteousness *as a human being*. That is, He actually did all the things a human must do to be a human being totally righteous before God. We call this the **active obedience** of Christ.

Certainly Jesus the Christ did not need any human righteousness for Himself—He was the holy God. However, the human race needs righteousness badly. By earning it for us, Christ gained both the right and the ability to impute (give) to us His earned righteousness. You will see this more thoroughly in the next chapter, but for now you want to remember it as part of Christ's humiliation.

The climax of the Lord's humiliation was His **passive obedience,** His death on the cross in submission to God the Father's will. On the cross, the Father poured out on Christ all the wrath of God that mankind deserved. In so doing, the punishment we all deserve was executed on Christ, just as the righteousness He earned He gives to us.

Exaltation

Following His death on the cross, Jesus rose from the dead in triumph. He had earned eternal life as a human being, then absorbed the punishment human beings deserve—effectively swapping with man what each had duly earned. In response to Christ's obedience in working salvation for man, the Father exalted Him above all creation. We don't know what the difference is, if any, between the Son's

glory in the past and His present glory, but we know that He has received additional special honor for actually carrying out salvation's plan. He who endured humiliation now is exalted to God the Father's right hand, the place of highest honor (Phil. 2:9-11).

Conclusion

There can be no Christianity without the unique divine-human Son of God. As His person is unique, so is His work unique. Jesus Christ is in Himself and by Himself the Savior. He initiated salvation, He accomplished all the necessary work, and He completed salvation for mankind. He was both holy deity and perfect humanity, and who He was enabled Him to do what he did—take all the punishment due for our sins while simultaneously giving us the righteousness He had earned. Only in Christ can there ever be salvation.

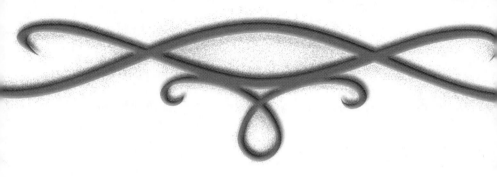

Hail, Thou Once-Despised Jesus!

John Bakewell, 1721-1819

Hail! Thou once-despised Jesus!
Hail, Thou Galilean King!
Thou didst suffer to release us;
Thou didst free salvation bring.
Hail, Thou agonizing Saviour,
Bearer of our sin and shame!
By Thy merits we find favor;
Life is given through Thy name.

Paschal Lamb, by God appointed,
All our sins on Thee were laid;
By almighty love anointed,
Thou hast full atonement made.
All Thy people are forgiven,
Through the virtue of Thy blood;
Opened is the gate of heaven,
Peace is made 'twixt man and God.

Worship, honor, power and blessing
Thou art worthy to receive;
Loudest praises, without ceasing,
Meet it is for us to give.
Help, ye bright angelic spirits,
Bring your sweetest, noblest lays;
Help to sing our Saviour's merits,
Help to chant Immanuel's praise!

CHAPTER FIVE

The Salvation Which Is in Jesus Christ

5

Memory Verses: Romans 3:21-28

Overheard:

Dexter: Hey, did you hear that Dan <u>got saved</u>?

Kenda: Who, Dan Garner? No, I hadn't heard. When?

D: Sunday night, when Pastor gave that long invitation about <u>giving your heart to Jesus</u>.

K: Wow. I never thought Dan would be one to <u>trust Christ</u>. He's always been so cold and hard about spiritual things.

D: Well, I guess it goes to show that <u>God can save</u> anybody.

K: I heard that Rand talked to him once about <u>accepting Jesus into his heart</u>, but Dan just laughed at him and walked away.

D: Do you think someone like that is really <u>hearing God's voice</u>, but they just don't like to admit it?

K: Maybe. But I remember before I was <u>born again</u> that I really didn't care anything about Christ.

D: I don't remember what it was like before I <u>believed in Jesus</u>; I was too little. I hear about people who didn't <u>find Jesus</u> until they were old, and I just can't think what that was like for them.

K: Why does God let people get old without <u>being saved</u>?

GET THE BIG PICTURE

I. Who Is Responsible for Salvation?
   A. Introduction to the Problem
   B. The Two Views of Responsibility
II. Individual Doctrines of Salvation
   A. Justification
   B. Sanctification
   C. Glorification
   D. Adoption
   E. Regeneration
   F. Redemption
   G. Propitiation
   H. Expiation

Everything in the overheard conversation has to do with salvation. Salvation is the Bible's most encompassing word for what Jesus Christ brought to the human race. The previous chapter explored the person and work of Christ. This chapter will examine what Christology means for you and me and everyone else on earth. Christ did what He did to save us, or to "bring us salvation." The study of salvation is called **soteriology** from *soteria*, meaning "salvation," and *logia*, meaning "study of."

Have you ever considered how much jargon some Christians use? If you didn't go to church as a child, you may have found it confusing. Maybe you still do. But even many people who talk in "Christian jargon" don't know precisely what it means.

"Are they speaking Chinese, Grandpa?"

"No, it's Christianese."

If we read the overheard conversation carefully, another problem with understanding salvation becomes apparent. Dexter and Kenda seem unaware of the problem, as many Christians are. They automatically refer to salvation with phrases like "Jesus saved him" and "he trusted Christ" or "God forgave him" and "he asked Jesus into his heart." They may use these interchangeably without realizing that they seem to contradict each other.

When Mike was saved, exactly what happened? Did God save him or did he trust Jesus? Both, of course, but which one happened first? Did Mike trust Jesus, and then God saved him? Or did God enable him to believe, and then Mike trusted God? Perhaps these seem to be pedantic questions, but they reflect the difficulty of understanding the most important moment of life. We must address them. As a Christian, you should be explaining salvation for the rest of your life, regardless of your career or social circle.

We have two major topics to tackle in the study of soteriology. First, we will look at the problem of who is responsible for salvation. Dexter and Kenda used interchangeable phrases that seem to make God responsible sometimes and people responsible sometimes. What does the Bible say? Second, we will look at the individual terms used in Scripture to describe salvation. Together they paint a picture of an event so transcendent of natural human experience, human language strains to convey it.

Who Is Responsible for Salvation?

Introduction

Salvation is as cosmic as eternity and as detailed as your individual soul. Consequently, we have to look at salvation both broadly and narrowly. We have to keep in mind what God has done for everybody in the past, what happens at the time a person is converted, and what goes on following conversion.

You have the challenge of balancing in your mind that God's preparatory work applies to the whole race and to every individual, including you. God's work applies to the race in a different manner than it applies to you, but it is still the same work. Clear as concrete? Let's use two diagrams to contrast the different aspects of salvation.

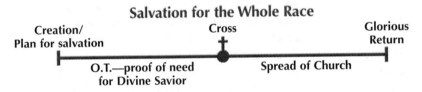

Salvation for the Whole Race

Creation/ Plan for salvation — Cross — Glorious Return

O.T.—proof of need for Divine Savior — Spread of Church

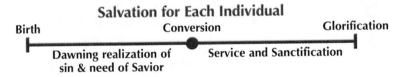

Salvation for Each Individual

Birth — Conversion — Glorification

Dawning realization of sin & need of Savior — Service and Sanctification

1. When God planned salvation, you were part of His plan.

2. Christ's work on the cross is applied to you, personally, at your conversion.

3. Your future glorification is not complete until God establishes His eternal kingdom with you in it.

While these parallels must not be overblown, they are very significant. The salvation plan for humankind is what makes possible your personal salvation. Keep that in mind as we study God's initiative in salvation.

Be cautious when exploring the doctrine of salvation. A remarkable feature of salvation is that its essentials are simple enough for a child to understand but its details defy the comprehension of the sharpest theologian. You encounter issues very difficult to reconcile. Facts seem to contradict; logical conclusions seem unacceptable. Remember that the Trinity and the dual nature of Christ are impossible to really understand. They are beyond us, in the realm that only God's mind inhabits. Certain parts of soteriology are the same way.

In this first section we will confront a controversial topic—election. Your challenge is to decide what the Bible actually says without being driven to conclusions by preconceived notions. Be confident that the Bible will not disappoint you. Given time to learn and digest everything it says about salvation, you will be a much stronger and happier Christian.

God planned the whole redemption of man from the very beginning. The Bible tells us that He chose believers in Christ before the world began (Eph. 1:4). Christians are elected (chosen or selected) according to the foreknowledge of God (I Pet. 1:2). **Foreknowledge** means "front knowledge," what is known beforehand. Those whom God foreknew He predestined to come to Christ (Eph. 1:4-5). **Predestine** means to establish something's destiny before it occurs. Finally, God calls those He predestines to come to Himself on the basis of the work of Christ.

Do you see the difficulty? Consider and ask yourself, if God chose who was going to be saved, why didn't He just choose everybody? Doesn't He want everyone to be saved?

Some illustrate this problem with a tree. Imagine a giant oak tree. You can see the leaves, the branches coming together, and the massive trunk going down to the ground. But even though you know there is more to the tree—the sprawling root system is as extensive as the branches—you cannot see any more. The root system anchors the tree in the ground and provides its

The Order of Decrees

Certain theologians have made an issue out of the order in which God *decided to* create man, allow the Fall of man, and redeem man through Christ. In other words, did he decide before creating man that man would fall and that He would redeem Him? Did He decide that He would redeem man only after He decided man would fall? This sequence is called the order of decrees, and it has to do with the workings of the mind of God before He created the world.

"So what?" you may ask. Well, the question is whether or not God *intended* for man to sin so that He could save (some) people. The Bible offers no direct input about the order of decrees. While it may be a legitimate question in theology, the order of decrees can become an "unlearned question" that only causes division. It should not occupy excessive time or become a basis for fellowship.

nourishment, but just by looking you wouldn't know it was there. The mysteries of God's redemptive plan are like the oak tree. We can see parts of it, but we cannot see the basis for it. God's mind is vastly beyond our meager understanding.

Look up each of the following Scripture passages and summarize it in your own words. Then compare the passages in Column A to the passages in Column B.

A	B
Isa. 45:22 _____	Eph. 1:3-6 _____
_____	_____
John 3:14-17_____	I Pet. 2:9 _____
_____	_____
_____	Rom. 8:30 _____
I Tim. 2:3-6 _____	_____
_____	II Tim. 1:9 _____
_____	_____
II Pet. 3:9 _____	II Thess. 2:13-14 _____
_____	_____

What do the passages in the first column imply? They imply that God wants all people to be saved by turning from their sins to God. What does the second column imply? It implies that God chooses who will be saved before they are saved and then brings those chosen people to Himself.

If we think through the ramifications of each of these columns, they don't seem to reconcile very well. How can both implications be true? Yet, all of these passages are in the Bible. Peter and Paul (Paul wrote Timothy, Ephesians, and Thessalonians) have passages in both columns. Were the men whom the Holy Spirit used to write the Bible contradicting one another, or even themselves? If so, then the Holy Spirit also contradicted Himself.

You are now face to face with a classic problem in Christian theology. From the early centuries of the Church, Christians have wrestled with how God could "elect" people to salvation but still call on the whole world to repent and be saved. The Bible tells clearly that God hasn't called everyone to salvation and that many people will not be saved (Rev. 20; Luke 16). Don't worry if this quandary is disconcerting; many good Christian people have worried over it for a long time.

That many Christians have trouble with this problem should tell us something up front—that is, that both sides have valid arguments. The two columns of passages above compress the evidence, but there are many more verses and logical reasons on both sides. Consequently we will not jump to conclusions, nor will we belittle or besmirch either side. We want to honestly examine the relevant Scriptures and contemplate exactly what God said and why He said it.

Keep in mind that God could have presented the Scripture without leaving any room for this problem. Even if one or the other side is correct and God means for us to realize it, He could have made it clearer. God could have kept all ambiguity away, either by providing an answer or by omitting part of the data. He has not done so.

God has allowed certain difficulties to be in the Bible. We are discussing only one of several. The Trinity, for example, is another. These problems of interpretation, as they are called, may be there because we humans are unable to grasp any more of the truth than has been revealed. If we are limited in understanding, then God has revealed as clearly as He can the truths of salvation. Also, they may be there because God tests us with them. If He could have revealed more but did not, then He wishes to try our faith and stimulate us to more earnest, sustained Bible study.

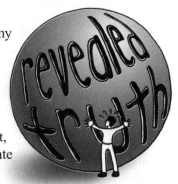

It may be that both reasons undergird the chief problem of soteriology—how to reconcile God's election to salvation with the fact that many people will never be saved. Therefore, we proceed with two goals: first, a determination to be humble before the mysteries of God; second, a determination to embrace exactly what the Bible says on both sides.

To begin with, let's see what the Bible says about man's condition prior to salvation. We can see that God took the initiative in salvation, but what does it take for a man to respond? Scripture says that the human heart is completely wicked (Jer. 17:9), man cannot do good (Rom. 3:12), and man is spiritually dead due to his stubborn rebellion against the Lord (Eph. 2:1-3). It would make sense, then, that God does all the work in salvation and man has essentially nothing to do with it. After all, if there is an absolute bent to evil, how can the mind make the righteous choice to trust God for salvation? How can he even understand it unless God actually makes him able to?

Column B above fits nicely with this data. Logically, if God decides in advance who will be saved, then we have nothing to do with salvation. As Scripture says, we have no cause to brag or take credit for our salvation (Eph. 2:8-9). God did it; He chose us, He loved us, He saved us. We must fall before Him in gratitude and give Him all the glory.

However, the state of unsaved man does not seem to fit the first column very well. Why not? Because if man has nothing to do with his own salvation, and God has to do all the saving, then why do the Column A passages say that God wants all men to be saved? If we logically extend the first column to understand the nature of man, it follows that God offers salvation to everyone but that only those who want it are saved. That is, those who respond favorably to the offer, who "believe" or "accept salvation" are saved.

Does the Bible ever teach that human beings must willfully choose salvation in order to be saved? See John 3:16; Romans 10:9-13; Revelation 22:17. All of these passages imply that people must choose salvation. If people are responsible to believe God, then it isn't so difficult to see why many people will never be saved. It is their failure, not God's choice. God did everything necessary to enable the salvation of mankind. It remains to man only to believe and be saved. But since so many are lost in sin and refuse to repent of their sin, not all human beings will be saved.

Are you adequately confused, or shall we continue? Step back from this discussion and consider where the problem comes from. The problem arises from the implications, or logical consequents, of the biblical data. To say it differently, we get into trouble when we go beyond what the passages actually say to what the logical implications of these passages are. The passages themselves teach certain truths that do not themselves contradict, but their logical consequents do.

Let's line these passages up with their consequents to see the whole situation at a glance. Say we first take the passages teaching that man is completely dead in sin and thus can do nothing to take part in his salvation (Rom. 3:12; Jer. 17:9; Eph. 2:1-3). When we summarize them in one sentence, this is the result:

Man is totally dead in sin.

Add to the previous sentence a summary of the passages teaching that God is wholly responsible for choosing who gets saved and for doing all the work of salvation Himself (Column B). Nothing about the people He chooses is innately worth His trouble because we are all dead in sin. His choice lies wholly in Himself. He has no conditions on His choice, but He doesn't choose everyone.

God unconditionally chooses who will be saved.

Now we deal with the logical consequents of these two statements. First, it is logical that God's plan of salvation never

Title Fight

DID YOU KNOW?

The two counterpoint positions represented by Columns A and B have names drawn from their historic roots. It must be remembered that the problem predates the men its parties are named for by hundreds of years. Furthermore, neither of these men necessarily espoused everything currently associated with the –ism based on his name. Both men appear to have been devoted ministers of God and are not to be blamed for the excesses of their followers.

John Calvin—Swiss reformer and pastor in Geneva. Calvin's teachings form the basis of **Calvinism**, the position corresponding to Column A. Calvin was opposing the Roman Catholic Church, which focused to an unbiblical extreme on human efforts.

James Arminius—Dutch theologian and pastor a generation after Calvin. His systematized response to extreme Calvinism is now called **Arminianism,** corresponding to Column B. He believed contemporary Calvinists had dangerously reduced the role of human responsibility in salvation.

Each of these systems appeared in an atmosphere of opposition. Their opponents held extremes of the opposite position. Whenever an enemy propagates an extreme, you are likely to react too far against it.

---

included the whole world at all, but only God's chosen. Therefore, Christ's death was only for those who would believe.

Christ died only for God's elect.

Furthermore, if human will has nothing to do with salvation, then it doesn't matter whether we want to be saved or not. In fact, no one wants to be saved until God makes him want salvation, so when God saves people, He chooses regardless of their resistance.

God saves by grace despite resistance.

Now we face the problem. We have four statements, but only the first two come directly from the Bible. The latter two are logical consequents of the first, but the Bible never says either one.

That was the result of starting with the Column B passages and reasoning forward. What happens if we start with the passages in Column A and work forward? First, look at Matthew 23:37;

Luke 10:13; and Hebrews 6:4-6. It is evident from these passages that God's grace can be resisted by rebellious human beings. To summarize,

People can resist God's saving grace.

Next, look at the passages that say that God wants everyone to be saved (Column A). It appears clear enough that Christ's death was for the whole human race.

Christ died for the entire human race.

Now what are the logical implications of these two scriptural statements? If Christ died for all, people can potentially resist grace, and many people won't be saved, it makes sense that God has placed a major condition on His choice of salvation—belief. He may choose you, but you have to choose Him back in order to be saved.

God chooses people to be saved on the condition that they believe.

If this sentence is true, we come to conclude that man has inside himself the ability to respond to God's offer of salvation. Man may be wholly sinful, but he can't be quite dead or completely helpless. All men have the ability to choose salvation in Christ.

Human beings are able to choose to believe.

When we take the first four statements and compare them to the latter four statements, we find something very interesting. Have you noticed their relationship? They correspond to each other in reverse order.

In each quartet of statements, the first two arise from direct Bible statements and the next two are logical consequents of the first two. Each pair of logical consequents corresponds to the direct Bible statements in the other column. The Bible statements do not contradict each other directly, but their logical consequents contradict the opposing Bible statements.

Where we end up depends on which passages of the Bible we start with. If we start with passages on humanity's dead condition and God's election of the saved (Column B), we logically conclude that Christ died only for the elect and that God saves the ones He chooses regardless of any opposition from them. On the other hand, if we start with the passages indicating that people can resist and refuse God's grace and that Christ died for the whole race, then we logically conclude that God conditions His election on belief and that people are able and responsible to choose salvation.

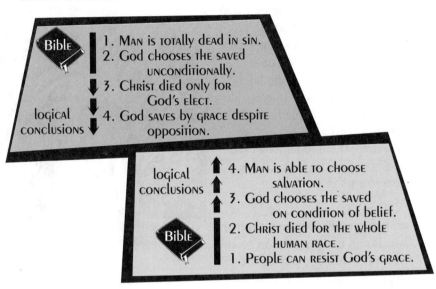

In light of all of this data, Christians should not be hasty in assuming either of these positions or in criticizing those who hold the opposite view. You should not necessarily abandon this problem as unsolvable, but you must be aware of the arguments on both sides. The problem isn't imagined. It is real, and it must be treated with humility.

What do you personally do to know you are saved? All these doctrines can be unsettling because they deal with my eternal destiny. But the beauty of God's Word is that it is easy to understand what I have to do to be saved, even if it's hard to understand everything that goes into my salvation.

You and I have to trust Jesus Christ for salvation. If I do that, then I know God has chosen me because everyone who chooses salvation has been chosen by God. I don't need to worry about it. The paradox should not cause you to worry about your salvation (What if God didn't pick me?) because the Bible never approaches us that way. It confronts every human being with the command to trust Christ.

Individual Doctrines of Salvation

Salvation is a complex event—many things happen at the point of conversion, others happen after conversion, and some await the time when the believer is with Christ in eternity. The Bible explains these events in different places; we will draw them together to see just how great a work God has done for us in salvation.

Don't let yourself be bored with this stuff. All the technical words can make salvation seem like a dry subject, but we are talking about things that happen to *you*. Understanding them makes you realize just what dramatic, costly, and intricate work God does for you. Not only does my gratitude to God increase when I ponder the doctrines of salvation, but it actually changes my behavior. Salvation is the basis for everything in life—every action, every word, even every thought is different because of salvation.

Justification

"Shall not the Judge of all the earth do right?" Abraham asked the Lord (Gen. 18:25). Abraham recognized that God is the ultimate judge. Remember that Christ's office as king incorporates the authority of a judge. We all face the courtroom of this divine judge. As sinners, we are in one sense already condemned by God the Judge and in another sense facing condemnation by Him after we die.

Is it right that God should condemn us for our sins? We may think not because so many people who are not true Christians seem to be basically good. But the question of goodness depends on the standard we have to live up to. Naturally, we humans judge good and bad by our own standards, but the standard that matters is God's (Ps. 50:21). Next to Him, none of us is the least bit good or righteous. And our shortcoming is not just a matter of scale—we look bad only because God is *so* good. No, the fact is that, according to what God considers good and bad, we are completely bad.

In consequence, all mankind stands before God guilty and condemned (Rom. 3:19). God is completely justified in condemning us; in fact, He can't do anything else because it would violate His own nature. God's justice repulses us only when we fail to realize how miserably wicked we really are.

Are you glad that God will not tolerate the least bit of evil, even if it means you are guilty of great sin? You should be, because God's justice guarantees that He will allow no evil in His presence at all (Ps. 5:4; Rev. 21:27). With Him will be only goodness, righteousness, joy, and peace without end. All it takes to live with Him forever is a life of perfect righteousness in His sight.

However, it is impossible for a human to be right with God (Rom. 3:23). Hence the need for the work of Christ, which we studied in the previous chapter. When the actively earned righteousness of Christ is given to us, God declares us righteous in His own sight. This declaring of righteousness is termed **justification.** God declares us to be just, or righteous. We are not *really* righteous, but God rules that we are righteous, due to the fact that Christ's righteousness is legally "given" to us (Rom. 3:21-26).

Christ	Man
• earned righteousness	• earned punishment
• received our sins though He was righteous	• received His righteousness though we are sinful
• received our punishment though He was innocent	• received His mercy though we are guilty

It is important to remember that justification has nothing to do with a change in us. The change is in our legal status. Imagine you are charged with murder by a foreign country, tried in absentia (you aren't there at the trial), and sentenced to death. You live on as you always have in your own country, but (in that other country) your legal status is changed. Now suppose new evidence arises in that country's investigation and they realize you are innocent. The court acquits you. Still nothing happened to you, but your status returns to "clean."

What has changed? If you visit that country, you can tour sites, eat in restaurants, and potentially even live there. If you had gone there when you were wanted, you'd have found yourself arrested and possibly executed.

Our situation is somewhat as if God has found us guilty of capital crimes, but we have fled from Him to a foreign country. We cannot be with Him either in heaven or eternity because we are "wanted" by Him. The problem is that we actually live in God's territory. He has entrusted the world to mankind temporarily, but still it is His. And we cannot avoid His justice forever, for we must go before Him after death. The one and only way to avoid the death penalty we deserve is to have our legal status changed—justification.

A major historical controversy concerns the difference between justification by faith alone and justification by faith plus something else. It should be apparent that when we observe in the Bible that justification is by faith, it implies that faith is the only way to justification. If something else were needed, the Bible would say justification is by faith and X.

It takes loose playing with language to agree that justification is by faith while meaning that it takes faith with something else.

It should be enough to affirm that justification is through faith, but it is necessary to specify faith *alone.*

Most often the element added to faith is works, meaning good acts done to merit reward. But saying that justification is by faith plus works effectively denies that it is by faith. Faith is not an ingredient; it is trust. If works justify me, then by definition I must put part of my faith (trust) in those works. Thus, my faith isn't in Jesus Christ, but divided into my works.

Sanctification

The next doctrine of salvation is **sanctification.** *Sanctify* means "to set apart" or "to make holy." A holy thing or place is set apart for a specific religious purpose. *Sacred* is a synonym for holy. The word has many meanings, but we are concerned only with those that relate to salvation.

Sanctification itself has three phases. The first is **positional sanctification** (I Cor. 1:30). At the point of conversion, God sanctifies a believer from the world. In a sense this is step one in a process, and in a sense it is a completed action. A converted believer is literally different. Whereas justification concerns only God's view of a process, sanctification results in something different about the believer.

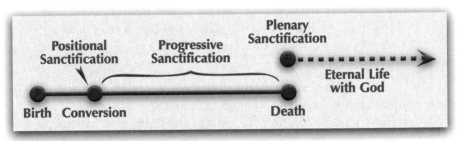

After positional sanctification, the process of sanctification begins through which a believer becomes less given to sin and more inclined to godly righteousness (I Thess. 4:1-3; Phil. 1:6). We call this phase **progressive sanctification,** because the believer makes progress in becoming more like God and less like the unconverted sinner. Sanctification can be seen as a cooperative work in which the believer learns God's Word, develops holy habits, and makes careful choices while the Spirit of God provides the power to change and grow. The Spirit is wholly to be credited for growth in grace (II Cor. 3:18).

The third and final phase of sanctification comes when the believer is reunited with Christ and all his sin is removed. To use a third 'p' we can call this event **plenary sanctification,** or complete sanctification. What is begun at conversion is completed, the goal of salvation fulfilled.

Glorification

A broader term for what happens when the believer joins Christ is the exaltation of the believer to the position Christ earned for him—enthroned with Christ at God's side, ruling over all creation, endowed with eternal life. Theologians often refer to this exaltation as **glorification.**

You may say something like, "I don't feel too glorious, and the Christians around me don't look very glorious, either." True, no doubt, but that is why we need glorification revealed to us in the Bible. A Christian is like the prince in *The Prince and the Pauper;* he looks to everyone like a normal boy, poor and lowly. But in fact he is royalty, bearing by rights the authority of a king's son. Think about that the next time you are beaten down or depressed by life's burdens. You and all the children of God around you are princes and princesses of a higher order than any human dynasty. God glorifies you.

We should notice that glorification becomes partly true at the point of conversion but is not realized until the next life. However, just like with sanctification, the present and future occurrences are part of the same reality. That is to say, the same way you will be glorified someday is already partly in effect immediately after conversion. Full sanctification and glorification are not in a different dimension from the life you know now. You are already set apart from sin, already progressing to the total holiness you will have in heaven, and already granted a high and exalted position in heaven. You just aren't there yet.

Adoption

Scripture calls us children of God. We are His children both by birth and by adoption. **Adoption** is a legal term as well as a familial one. In the first century A.D., when the New Testament writers were picking the various words to describe salvation, adoption had two meanings. First, it was used to indicate the acceptance of a child into a family not his by birth. Second, it referred to the elevation of a young man to full adult status.

Both elements picture salvation. We are adopted at the point of conversion into God's family (Gal. 4:5-7). We were foreign born, you might say, but God took us as His own. In the future, when we are united with Christ in eternal life, we will receive "adoption" to the complete status due to God's children (Rom. 8:23).

The two images of adoption represent two aspects of salvation. Salvation is both a gift from God to us and a legal right resulting from birth into God's family. Obviously no human son can be both natural and adopted, but spiritual children are both at once.

Regeneration

Perhaps the most vital image of salvation is regeneration (Titus 3:5). *Regenerated* literally means "born again." Unbelievers are spiritually dead. They cannot be merely healed; they must be made new. The spiritual nature is there, sensing the existence of divinity and often longing for it, but without the capability of knowing and walking with God. Sin has killed us, even before we die. Through regeneration, God makes us live even after we die.

John 3 is the paramount passage on regeneration. Christ implied to Nicodemus, a master teacher of the Jews, that he should have known about regeneration from the Old Testament alone. Christ said that new birth was by the Spirit and was necessary to entering the kingdom of God.

Redemption

Slavery was an established institution in the Roman world of the New Testament. Many people were slaves, though few wanted to be, naturally. One became a slave in various ways, but one way was through bankruptcy. If you borrowed heavily and then couldn't pay, your creditor could sell you as a slave to recoup his loss. If that happened, your father and mother might scrape together enough money to buy you back, or *redeem* you, and so spare you years in a stranger's barley fields. The image is of us, sinners who have lost our lives to slavery to sin, being redeemed by our Father at His own expense (Eph. 1:7). We are now His, free from sin, free to do right.

Propitiation

A controversial term relating to salvation is **propitiation,** a turning aside of wrath. (Propitiation is pronounced pro-*pish*-ee-ay-shun, not pro-*pitch*-ee-ay-shun.) As always, we have to carefully define the term. The English word *propitiation* generally means an appeasement of wrath, like a gift to mollify an angry god. The New Testament word emphasizes the deflection of wrath onto something else (I John 4:10; Rom. 3:25). It refers to the sacrificed animal that supposedly substituted for the worshiper.

Some people dislike this word because they deny that God could be angry with us. But He is (Ps. 7:11-12). I only deny God's wrath if I don't know or refuse to believe what the Bible teaches about my own sin. God's anger against my sins was intense. Nothing I could do would turn it away from me. Christ became the propitiation for my sins—He took my sin on Himself, and so absorbed all the punishment due for my sins. He thereby calmed the wrath of God that was directed at me.

Expiation

Christ did not merely take the punishment for my sins; He took away my sins. Christ did not become sinful, but He became sin for us (II Cor. 5:21). My sins are now removed from me and gone, because the wrath of God that destroyed them has been fully executed—not on me, even though they were my sins, but on Christ (John 1:29). The word used for the removal of sin from a sinner is **expiation,** or cleansing. In this word sin is pictured as dirt or filth that the Lord washes away.

Conclusion

These are the different elements of salvation. We have looked out over the great mystery of salvation, that God chooses us and yet we are still responsible to choose to be saved. We have considered the various elements of salvation, a complex work connecting Christ's work on the cross to you and me, the sinners. How can we do anything other than give Him our faith, love, and life?

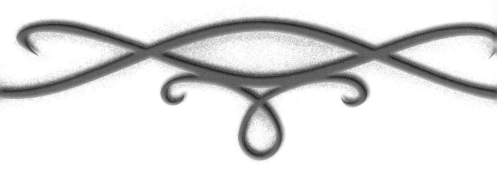

Jesus, Thy Blood and Righteousness

Nicolaus L. Zinzendorf, 1700-1760
Trans. by John Wesley, 1703-1791

Jesus, Thy blood and righteousness
My beauty are, my glorious dress;
'Midst flaming worlds, in these arrayed,
With joy shall I lift up my head.

Bold shall I stand in Thy great day,
For who aught to my charge shall lay?
Fully absolved through these I am,
From sin and fear, from guilt and shame.

Lord, I believe Thy precious blood,
Which, at the mercy seat of God,
Forever doth for sinners plead,
For me, e'en for my soul, was shed.

Lord, I believe were sinners more
Than sands upon the ocean shore,
Thou hast for all a ransom paid,
For all a full atonement made.

CHAPTER SIX

The Fulness of Him that Filleth All in All

6

Memory Verses: Ephesians 4:7, 11-16

If ye have heard of the dispensation of the grace of God which is given me to you-ward: how that by revelation he made known unto me the mystery; . . .That the Gentiles should be fellowheirs, and of the same body, and partakers of his promise in Christ by the gospel: whereof I was made a minister, according to the gift of the grace of God given unto me by the effectual working of his power. Unto me, who am less than the least of all saints, is this grace given, that I should preach among the Gentiles the unsearchable riches of Christ; and to make all men see what is the fellowship of the mystery, which from the beginning of the world hath been hid in God, who created all things by Jesus Christ. (Ephesians 3:2-3, 6-9)

The apostle Paul was a man whose life and ministry were characterized by the supernatural. He had experienced the glory of God in heaven, had been visited by an angel, had miraculously healed people of various maladies, and had cast out demons. Yet when he spoke of those experiences, they did not evoke from him the excitement and sense of privilege that pervades this quotation from Ephesians. And—amazingly—his words in Ephesians 3 refer to a work of God that all of us are privileged to enjoy every moment of our Christian experience. In these verses the apostle reveals that *salvation is more than individual.* The Father has so planned His saving work that it is experienced with others in a community. Paul makes it clear that this community of joy and faith is not a Jewish institution, like Israel in the Old Testament. When Christ died, He removed the distinction between Jew and Gentile, "having abolished in his flesh the enmity . . . for to make in himself of twain one new man" (Eph. 2:15). This community is a new creation of God—*the church,* "the fulness of him that filleth all in all" (Eph. 1:23).

GET THE BIG PICTURE

I. What Is the Church?
II. Why Does the Church Exist?
III. What Does the Church Do?

What Is the Church?

"The tyranny of the Church was broken when Martin Luther publicly questioned its authority." "Church was a great blessing today." "I can't wait to move into our new church." The word *church* is certainly not unfamiliar to us. However, we do not read far in the New Testament before we realize that the Bible's use of the word differs significantly from our own. This difference does not require that we change the way we use the word in our daily conversations. But it does indicate that if we want to understand the Bible's teaching in this matter, we must take time to understand what "church" meant to the biblical writers as they penned Scripture.

The Word *Ekklesia*

The Greek word translated "church" in our English Bibles is the word *ekklesia* (ek klay SEE uh). Like our word "church," it has several different meanings. None of them, however, correspond to the meanings in the three quoted sentences that begin the previous paragraph. Scholars generally agree that *ekklesia* is used in three different ways in the New Testament. First, it sometimes refers to a gathering of people who have met together to accomplish some common goal. It is not

In first century Greek, ekklesia *could refer to any assembly of people—even the unruly crowd at Ephesus.*

surprising, therefore, that the citizens of Ephesus who assembled in the city's theater are referred to as an *ekklesia* (Acts 19:32, 39, 41; KJV "assembly").

1) AN ASSEMBLY OF PEOPLE

EKKLESIA

2) THE COMMUNITY OF THE SAVED

3) THIS COMMUNITY MANIFESTED IN A SPECIFIC PLACE

This meaning, however, accounts for only a handful of the occurrences of *ekklesia* in the New Testament. In many cases the word communicates a meaning that apparently originated with the teaching of Christ and His apostles: *the whole community of persons who have been reconciled to God by trusting in the finished work of Jesus Christ.* Our Lord used this sense of *ekklesia* when He predicted, "I will build my church; and the gates of hell shall not prevail against it" (Matt. 16:18). This usage does not view the church as divided by locality or time. According to this meaning, there is only one church, and it includes all believers in Christ, both those on earth and those in heaven. The author of Hebrews uses the word in this sense when he refers to the *ekklesia* as the "church of the firstborn, which are written in heaven" (Heb. 12:23). This meaning dominates the book of Ephesians. The apostle Paul reveals that after His resurrection, Jesus Christ was made "the head over all things to the church" (Eph. 1:22). A couple chapters later he prays that God the Father would be glorified "in the church by Christ Jesus throughout all ages, world without end" (3:21). In Ephesians 4, speaking of the church as the body of Christ, Paul asserts, "There is one body, and one Spirit . . . one Lord, one faith, one baptism, one God and Father of all" (vv. 4-6). And in chapter 5, he exhorts husbands to love their wives, "even as Christ also loved the church, and gave himself for it" (v. 25).

Often in the New Testament, *ekklesia* is used in a third sense. It can refer to the community of God's people as it is manifested

in a particular locality. When Paul addresses the believers living in Corinth, he writes, "Unto the church of God which is at Corinth, to them that are sanctified in Christ Jesus" (I Cor. 1:2). This was the meaning that Paul had in mind when he spoke of "all the churches of the Gentiles" (Rom. 16:4) and when he referred to "the churches of Judaea which were in Christ" (Gal. 1:22). And, certainly, this meaning is reflected in Colossians where the apostle exhorts the believers to greet "Nymphas, and the church which is in his house" (Col. 4:15).

We do not *go to* church—we *are* the church.

From this evidence we should learn two lessons. First, the word "church" in the New Testament always refers to *people*—not to places or things. Biblically speaking, the church is not a building, an organization, or a particular weekly event. Almost always in the New Testament, it refers to the community of those who have trusted Christ and are together being matured by God's Spirit. Therefore, according to Scripture, we do not *go to* church—we *are* the church.

Second, examining the use of *ekklesia* in Scripture should remind us that the church is a unity. Throughout the world today there are thousands of churches, but these many groups are simply manifestations of the one church of Jesus Christ. As Paul stated, "There is one body" (Eph. 4:4). The people that we meet with and minister with every week are not our only obligation as members of Christ's church. The church that worships two hours away is also the church of God—as are the thousands of churches scattered throughout the world. We are one with them as well, and they are our brothers and sisters in the Lord. If they have remained true to the gospel in their teaching and behavior, we should endeavor to fellowship with them and minister to them as much as possible. Sadly, as members of local churches, we often slip into an attitude of competition and resentment

toward other local churches. Sometimes we justify our negativism by scrutinizing other assemblies and judging them by standards we are unwilling to apply to our own church. Such attitudes grieve the Spirit of God. Christ's charge that we love one another as He loved us (John 13:34) applies not only to those in our own immediate fellowship. It applies just as surely to every member of

John Wycliffe (d. 1384), often called the Morning Star of the Reformation, shook England's confidence in the authority of the Pope by asserting that the church of Jesus Christ was universal and invisible. Wycliffe proclaimed that God alone made men and women members of Christ's body and that no pope or bishop had the knowledge or the authority to declare someone part of the church or to exclude them. Since Christ is the head of the church, Wycliffe declared, "No man should follow the pope, nor even any of the saints of heaven, except as they follow Christ." Recognizing that believers throughout England could not understand how to follow Christ without the Scripture, he produced the first complete translation of the Bible in English. Despite severe persecution, John Wycliffe died in peace in 1384. Infuriated by his damaging ministry, the Church of Rome exhumed Wycliffe's remains in 1428. In so doing, his enemies only

reinforced what he had labored to proclaim—God alone admits individuals into His church. No man has the authority to bar another's entrance. Although his bones were burned and the ashes scattered in a nearby stream, Wycliffe himself was unharmed, safe as a member of the church triumphant.

His church throughout the world. Only by nourishing and developing such an attitude, can we participate effectively with Christ in His worldwide work of preparing for Himself "a glorious church, not having spot, or wrinkle, or any such thing" (Eph. 5:27).

The Church as the Body of Christ

Throughout his epistles, Paul speaks of the church as the body of Christ. This revelation provides rich encouragement for the people of God who are willing to meditate on the details of New Testament doctrine. Learning how it is that believers become members in the body of Christ and comprehending the implications of that membership can and ought to be a life-changing experience.

Placement in Christ's Body—the Baptism of the Spirit

The coming of the Holy Spirit on all believers was an event greatly anticipated in the history of divine revelation. God, through Joel, prophesied some eight centuries before Christ, "I will pour out my spirit upon all flesh" (Joel 2:28). When John the Baptist prepared the multitudes for the coming of Christ's ministry, he declared, "I indeed have baptized you with water: but he [Jesus Christ] shall baptize you with the Holy Ghost" (Mark 1:8). The importance of this prophecy is demonstrated by the fact that all four Gospels mention this statement from Christ's forerunner (Matt. 3:11; Luke 3:16; John 1:33).

The Lord also taught that He was the source of this blessing. On one occasion, He announced to a large crowd, "He that believeth on me, as the scripture hath said, out of his belly shall flow rivers of living water" (John 7:38). Then the Gospel writer explains, "This spake he of the Spirit, which they that believe on him should receive" (v. 39). The night before He was crucified, He spoke of the divine Spirit as "the Comforter": "I will pray the Father, and he shall give you another Comforter, that he may abide with you for ever" (John 14:16). And after His resurrection, Christ told His followers to remain in Jerusalem and "wait for the promise of the Father, which . . . ye have heard of me. For John truly baptized with water; but ye shall be baptized with the Holy Ghost not many days hence" (Acts 1:4-5).

Only a few days later, on the day of Pentecost, the Lord's followers were unmistakably "all filled with the Holy Ghost" (Acts 2:4). As they miraculously testified to the power of the risen Christ, a large crowd gathered, and Peter announced, "This is that which was spoken by the prophet Joel; and it shall come to pass in the last days, saith God, I will pour out of my Spirit upon all flesh" (Acts 2:16-17; Joel 2:28). And as the book of Acts unfolds, Scripture repeatedly affirms that with God's gracious regeneration comes the pouring out of His Spirit on the believer's soul.

When we come to the epistles of Paul, we learn that this outpouring is intended to be more than an individual blessing. The baptism of the Spirit is the means by which we are made members of Christ's body. Paul told the Corinthian believers, "By one Spirit are we all baptized into one body, whether we be Jews or Gentiles, whether we be bond or free; and have been all made to drink [in] one Spirit" (I Cor. 12:13). This exquisite statement reveals that at

regeneration we experience a spiritual baptism that involves two different modes of baptism. God first pours out His Spirit on us, who comes to indwell us by our drinking Him in spiritually. Since that indwelling Spirit also lives within everyone else who is regenerated, this outpouring results in an immersion into a spiritual community. Therefore, by receiving the Holy Spirit at salvation, each one of us is made a part of the body of Jesus Christ. Though

"The . . . functions of the Spirit which pertain especially to the work of salvation may be classified under two general heads—the Holy Spirit as 'the Giver of life,' and the Holy Spirit as 'a sanctified Presence.' To the former belongs . . . the initial experience of salvation; to the latter, the baptism with the Spirit— a subsequent work by which the soul is made holy. This is known as entire sanctification. . . . While the child of God as an individual possesses life in Christ, there is in him also the 'carnal mind' or inbred sin, and this prevents him from entering fully into his New Testament privileges in Christ. . . . There must therefore be a purification from sin. . . . The *baptism* . . . refers to the act of purifying, or making holy."

the church is composed of millions of different people, we all form one body because we are all indwelled by the same Spirit. Just as every part of your physical body is connected to your brain through an elaborate network of nerve tissue, so all believers are spiritually connected to each other and to Christ (the head of the body) by the indwelling Spirit.

Implications of the Church as Christ's Body

When the New Testament refers to the church as the body of Christ, it does so to emphasize primarily two truths. First, it reminds us that **Christ is present in this world.** Our Lord never removed His presence from earth; He only changed the nature of His presence. Prior to His ascension, He was present in His physical body. At Pentecost He became present through His spiritual body, the church, "the fulness of him that filleth all in all" (Eph. 1:23). This terse yet important description by Paul in Ephesians 1 presents us with an interesting irony. Jesus Christ, as the exalted Son of God, fills all things (Eph. 4:10). Yet at the same time He occupies only one part of His spiritual body: He is its head. The rest of His body is "filled out" by the growing and maturing of the individual members of the church. As believers live and work for the Lord, they fill the earth with the special presence of the glorified Christ. They are "the fulness of him that filleth all in all."

This presence of Christ is an active presence, for the work of the church is simply an extension of the earthly ministry of Jesus. Luke begins his history of the early church by asserting this fact.

He refers to everything that Jesus did before His ascension as "all that Jesus *began* to do and teach" (Acts 1:1; emphasis added). Thus Luke implies that everything that follows in the book of Acts (and by implication in all of church history) is what Jesus *continues* to do and teach through His body, the Church.

Considering these truths should greatly encourage us in our efforts as Christians. Since we are part of Christ's spiritual body, our labors are the continuation of His earthly ministry. Sometimes we find ourselves longing to go back in time to those days when the Lord lived on this earth, teaching and working. We need to realize, however, that Christ is still present in this world teaching and working. What is perhaps most amazing is that He is continuing this work not simply among us but also *through us*. And since He is operating through this spiritual body and not His physical body, the works that He is accomplishing are greater than those He did two thousand years ago. The Lord prophesied this marvelous truth before He went to the cross: "He that believeth on me, the works that I do shall he do also; and greater works than these shall he do; because I go unto my Father" (John 14:12). Later in that same discourse, He expanded on this teaching by revealing, "It is expedient for you that I go away: for if I go not away, the Comforter will not come unto you; but if I depart, I will send him unto you" (John 16:7). By baptizing all believers with His Spirit, Christ fills the earth with His spiritual body, the church. Together the works of these Spirit-indwelled individuals are far greater than His first works because they circle the globe, whereas His former deeds were confined to a relatively small region.

> ## What Would You Say?
>
> When one examines the events of the day of Pentecost in the full context of Christ's teaching and the teaching of the apostles, it seems clear that the church and Israel are two different entities. At Pentecost something new began. It was not the continuation of Israel; it was the beginning of the church. Acts 7:38, however, seems to contradict this understanding. In the light of what we have discussed in this chapter, how would you explain this verse?

Second, Scripture refers to the church as Christ's body to emphasize that **believers need each other.** Perhaps the best expression of this truth is found in Paul's letter to the Romans: "We, being many, are one body in Christ, and every one members one of another" (Rom. 12:5). The church is composed of many different people who through their mutual dependence form one body. Just as in the human body the hand does not belong to itself but to the whole, so each one of us belongs to the entire body of Christ. Therefore, if the body of Christ is to function properly,

"Arg! That foot! Who needs it?!"

we must be community-focused, not self-focused. Paul admonished, "The members should have the same care one for another. And whether one member suffer, all the members suffer with it; or one member be honoured, all the members rejoice with it" (I Cor. 12:25-26).

Such a focus requires that we not envy the gifts and abilities of others. Instead, we should be content with the gifts that God has given us. For this reason Paul warns every believer "not to think of himself more highly than he ought to think; but to think soberly, according as God hath dealt to every man the measure of faith" (Rom. 12:3). At the same time, we must learn to take seriously our own role in the body of Christ, for no part of His body is unnecessary. It grows and enjoys good health only as the members participate "according to the effectual working in the measure of *every part*" (Eph. 4:16; emphasis added). Whenever one part fails to fulfill his task, progress in the whole is hindered.

The Church as the Temple of God

Scripture also speaks of the church as the temple of God. Centuries before Christ's ministry, God placed a special manifestation of His presence in the tabernacle of Moses (Exod. 40:34-38), and later in the temple built by Solomon (I Kings 8:10-11). During His earthly life, however, Jesus Christ revealed that God was going to change the way He ministered His special presence to His people. Conversing with the woman of Samaria about the

place where God was to be worshiped, Christ asserted, "The hour cometh, when ye shall neither in this mountain [Mount Gerazim], nor yet at Jerusalem, worship the Father" (John 4:21). That hour came when Christ baptized believers with the Holy Spirit at Pentecost. At that moment, rather than filling a physical structure with His special presence, God placed His Spirit inside each believer. Through the indwelling of that Spirit, God made the church His living temple—a temple not built with brick and mortar, but made of the souls of His Spirit-filled people. As Paul revealed, by the power of Jesus Christ the entire church "groweth unto an holy temple in the Lord: in whom ye also are builded together for an habitation of God through the Spirit" (Eph. 2:21-22).

Perhaps the most important implication for us to draw from this truth is the one that Paul pointed out to the Corinthian believers. After Paul planted the church at Corinth, the believers had become divided because different parts of the assembly preferred different ministers. Some were quite vocal that they thought Peter was a better minister than Paul, while others preferred Paul, and still others felt a preacher named Apollos was superior. Paul rebuked this partisan spirit by reminding them that as the church, they were part of God's temple: "Know ye not that ye are the temple of God, and that the Spirit of God dwelleth in you?" (I Cor. 3:16). Then he concluded, "Let no man glory in men" (v. 21).

As humans ministered to by humans, we too easily fall into the trap of exalting men in the service and worship of the church. We must remember, however, that no matter how much a particular believer blesses us spiritually, that believer is only an instrument— a servant of Christ. The Lord is actually the one blessing us and building us up together as "an habitation of God through the Spirit" (Eph. 2:22). Once we grasp the wonder of this doctrine, we will no longer be man-focused in our Christianity. We will realize that we do not gather on Sundays to hear a man. We gather to gaze on God and be changed by that vision. The God who filled the tabernacle with His special presence is the same God who dwells enthroned in the church. When we meet, we "are gathered together . . . with the power of our Lord Jesus Christ" in our midst (I Cor. 5:4). The joy and privilege of being part of the church is not found in the skill, abilities, or even spiritual stature of our church leaders. Our greatest blessing is that God is among us to be known and adored by us—the living stones of His living temple.

Why Does the Church Exist?

The Church's Primary Purpose—Worship

God made the church to worship Him by glorifying His name. When we hear the word "worship," we usually think of the act of singing, praying, or testifying publicly about God's greatness and goodness. These activities are certainly part of the church's worship. However, according to Paul's letter to the Ephesians— the key epistle revealing that glorifying God is the church's ultimate purpose—our worship of God includes much more than just those activities. Paul reveals that God called him to declare the doctrine of the church "to the intent that now unto the principalities and powers in heavenly places might be known by the church the manifold wisdom of God" (Eph. 3:10). The church glorifies God not just by what it does in its meetings. The church worships God by what it is.

The church *worships* *God* by what it is.

By existing according to God's design, the church displays the "manifold wisdom of God."

In Ephesians the truth about the church that Paul emphasizes is that "the Gentiles should be fellowheirs [with the Jews], and of the same body, and partakers of his promise in Christ by the gospel" (Eph. 3:6). If this truth seems unremarkable to us, it is only because we are far too young to appreciate the significance of the church in the history of God's dealings with mankind. We, however, are not the primary audience for this life of worship.

Angelic beings ("the principalities and powers in heavenly places") are the intended observers, and they are as old as the world itself (Job 1:6; 38:7).

They beheld the creation of man, and they no doubt watched in amazement as they saw God deal kindly, yet sternly, with our first parents in their sin. Rather than judging them, as He had Satan, He promised to reverse their sad condition through a descendant of Eve (Gen. 3:15). As the history of the fulfillment of this promise progressed, God revealed to one man, Abraham, that He would make from him a mighty nation (Gen. 12:1-3). For the next two thousand years the angels observed God developing Abraham's descendants into a nation, giving them His laws, revealing His character, and promising that the predicted descendant of Eve would one day come to them through Abraham's line.

Amazingly, however, when the promised one came, the nation rejected Him and had Him executed in humiliation. The horror with which the "principalities and powers" viewed those tragic events must have been unimaginable. Yet God's promised son of Eve arose from the dead and demonstrated that His unjust death was the essential component in God's plan for reversing the curse

131

of sin (Gen. 3:15; Luke 24:25-27; Rom. 16:20; Rev. 12:9-11). Christ's rejection by the Jews did not frustrate God's promise to Abraham either. It rather led to another stage in God's progressive fulfillment of His promise. He had predicted that through Abraham "shall all families of the earth be blessed" (Gen. 12:3). Through the Jews' rejection of Jesus, God threw open the door to His kingdom for "all families of the earth." After His ascension Christ poured out His Holy Spirit on both Jews and Gentiles, making His kingdom no longer a nationalistic entity but a spiritual one in which both Jews and Gentiles are "fellowheirs, and of the same body, and partakers of his promise in Christ by the gospel" (Eph. 3:6). This new creation—the church—is not God's angry response to the Jew's rejection of His Son. It is in every way the further outworking of His marvelous plan to deliver men and women from sin—even the Jews that despise Jesus Christ. Paul reveals that "salvation is come unto the Gentiles, for to provoke [the Jews] to jealousy," and this jealousy is intended to "save some of them" (Rom. 11:11, 14).

When Paul completed his extended consideration of the Jews' rejection of Christ and the church's role in God's plan, he concluded, "O the depth of the riches both of the wisdom and knowledge of God! how unsearchable are his judgments, and his ways past finding out!" (Rom. 11:33). We are on display before the angelic throng. Through us God evokes from them the supernatural praise that He deserves. Indeed, "the manifold wisdom of God" is incomparable, and we are the irrefutable proof.

The Church's Secondary Purposes

By referring to the following two purposes of the church as "secondary," we do not mean that these are unimportant. They are called secondary because Scripture seems to indicate that they exist to serve the ultimate purpose of declaring God's glory. Although they are not the ultimate purpose for which the church was created, they are essential because without them the church cannot glorify God. They are the chief means by which the church achieves its central goal of rendering to God the worship He deserves.

Evangelism

Evangelism is the act of declaring the gospel to the unconverted in the hope that they will repent and trust Christ for salvation. Our Lord placed great importance on this work of the church. Just before He ascended to heaven, He charged His disciples to testify of His person and work to a lost world. In that final charge He revealed that one purpose for the outpouring of His Holy Spirit was to enable them to evangelize: "Ye shall receive power, after that the Holy Ghost is come upon you: and ye shall be witnesses unto me" (Acts 1:8). Taken in context, this command implies that evangelism is the responsibility of all Christians, not church leaders only. Christ promised to give all believers the Holy Spirit so that they could be supernaturally enabled to testify of Him. On the day of Pentecost, the Spirit came not just on the apostles but also on the other men that had followed Christ, as well as the women (Acts 1:12-15; 2:1-4). And when they were filled, they all evangelized throughout Jerusalem.

The command in Acts 1:8 also clearly establishes for the church the extent of its evangelism—"unto the uttermost part of the earth." According to the Book of Acts, the first generation of the church fulfilled this command with amazing success. In a few decades they evangelized from Jerusalem to Rome. Since that time subsequent generations have continued this work with great success and sacrifice. Despite these efforts, however, the task is still incomplete. The "uttermost part" has not yet been reached, for there are still many people groups that have never heard the gospel. But even if every part of the earth had been reached, we would still be obligated to evangelize because the earth's population is not static. People are constantly leaving this world through death, and new arrivals are born every minute. Each new life—even those from believing parents—is tainted by sin and must embrace the gospel or be eternally lost. As members of His church, we are responsible to continue fulfilling the commission first given to the apostles: "Go ye therefore, and teach all nations" (Matt. 28:19; Mark 16:15; Luke 24:46-49).

Christ placed great emphasis on the church's work of evangelism because it is essential to the church's worship. There can be no testimony to the "manifold wisdom of God" without converts  being added to the church. For this reason, when Paul speaks of the church as God's temple, he does not refer to it as a completed edifice but as one under construction: "All the building fitly framed together groweth [is growing] unto an holy temple in the Lord" (Eph. 2:21). This work is to continue until Christ returns to judge the world and set up His kingdom. In fact, the apostle Peter indicates that the necessity of continued evangelism is the reason that the day of the Lord has not already come: "The Lord is not slack concerning his promise [of the coming day of the Lord], as some men count slackness; but is longsuffering to us-ward, not willing that any should perish, but that all should come to repentance" (II Pet. 3:9). Since the Lord has not returned, we may conclude that the temple is not yet finished. Many living stones still need to be placed, and God has called us to be the instruments by which Christ fits them into the structure.

Edification

In Scripture the word *edification* refers to the work of improving and strengthening the spiritual life of believers. The Bible teaches that God accomplishes this work in the church through the operation of **spiritual gifts,** special abilities imparted to believers by the Holy Spirit. Paul explains in Ephesians 4 that after Christ ascended to heaven, He "gave gifts unto men [believers]" (v. 8; Ps. 68:18). Again, if we place this explanation in the context of the book of Acts, it appears that Paul is referring to the day of Pentecost. When Christ baptized believers with His Spirit, He not only brought them into a single spiritual community, but He also gave each member—through the Holy Spirit's indwelling—special gifts to enable them to edify one another.

The New Testament discusses spiritual gifts primarily in four different passages: Romans 12:6-8; I Corinthians 12:4-11, 28-30; Ephesians 4:11; and I Peter 4:10-11. Of these passages the most helpful for our brief presentation is I Peter 4. In verse 10 of the apostle's treatment, he reveals two important facts about spiritual gifts: "As every man hath received the gift, even so minister the same one to another, as good stewards of the manifold grace of God." First, we must realize that every believer has received a spiritual gift. Therefore, edifying the saints is not a task for pastors and deacons only. Edification is everyone's duty. Second, possessing spiritual gifts makes each of us a steward, one who manages something for another person. These special endowments are not our own. God has given them to us as His chosen means of ministering His "manifold grace" to each member of the church.

In verse 11, Peter indicates the nature of these gifts by speaking of them in two general categories: "If any man speak, let him speak as the oracles of God; if any man minister [serve], let him do it as of the ability which God giveth." Spiritual gifts are special abilities that enhance believers' effectiveness in promoting spiritual well-being through *speaking* and *serving*. Gifts that pertain to speaking include preaching, teaching, evangelizing, and encouraging. Gifts of serving would include giving, administrating, and manual labor directed at meeting physical needs. In these activities believers must remember that they are only instruments. The one who uses a speaking gift should view himself as one of the "oracles of God." Those who have serving gifts should view their work as something that "God giveth." Whenever we lose sight of the fact that our giftedness is not our own, we hinder God's purpose in the operation of spiritual gifts. Peter concludes his treatment by stating that Christ has distributed these gifts "that God in all things may be glorified through Jesus Christ" (I Pet. 4:11).

Many believers have difficulty appreciating the importance of edification. To them evangelism is the essential activity of the church, and edification is significant only as it enables Christians to evangelize. Scripture, however, places great emphasis on edification. In fact, while the New Testament epistles say very little about evangelism, they are almost entirely devoted to discussing

edification. Perhaps the reason for this emphasis is that edification is logically prior to evangelism. Believers cannot evangelize unless they are first edified. Paul intimates this truth in Ephesians 4:12, where he reveals that God gifts the members of His church "for the perfecting of the saints, for the work of the ministry." One "work of the ministry" is evangelizing the lost, but before this work—or any work—can go forward it must be preceded by "perfecting the saints." Edification is also logically subsequent to evangelism, for evangelism without later acts of edification produces a weak and unstable church. Again, in Ephesians 4, Paul encourages believers to use their gifts for edification: "That we henceforth be no more children, tossed to and fro, and carried about with every wind of doctrine" (v. 14).

Just as Paul communicates the importance of evangelism by picturing the church as an incomplete temple, so he emphasizes edification by referring to the church as a growing body. The body of Christ has not yet reached the "measure of the stature of the fulness of Christ" (Eph. 4:13). His body is not yet full-grown. As each of us submits to the leading of God's Spirit and trusts Him to empower the gifts He has distributed, we will be used of God. We can bring health and maturity to the body through the working of Jesus Christ, "from whom the whole body fitly joined together and compacted by that which every joint supplieth, according to the effectual working in the measure of every part, maketh increase of . . . itself in love" (Eph. 4:16).

What Does the Church Do?

To this point, our treatment of the biblical teaching regarding the church has been essentially abstract. We have discussed definitions of the church and considered the general purposes for which the church was created. We must now consider the practical aspects of the Bible's teaching. The following paragraphs survey the specific activities that the church is to engage in. Scripture presents these as the God-ordained means of evangelizing the lost, edifying the saints, and glorifying God.

Ministry of the Word

Shortly after recording that momentous day of Pentecost, the book of Acts gives us a telling snapshot of life in the early church: "And they continued stedfastly in the apostles' doctrine and fellowship, and in breaking of bread, and in prayers" (Acts 2:42). As this list indicates, one of the most important regular activities of the church is the ministry of the Word. Later in Acts, the busyness of other legitimate church duties began to crowd out the apostles' attempts to teach and preach. Because of these growing pressures, they instituted the office of deacon, explaining, "It is not reason [desirable] that we should leave the word of God, and serve tables" (Acts 6:2). Paul likewise emphasized the importance of the public ministry of the Word. He told Timothy to read the Scripture in the meetings of the church, to use it in exhorting God's people, and to teach its doctrines (I Tim. 4:13; II Tim. 4:2). The purpose of this regular ministry was not only to edify believers but also to evangelize the lost (II Tim. 4:5).

To Paul, it was not enough simply to minister Scripture with a sincere heart. He believed that the Word had to be handled correctly. Therefore, he commanded Timothy to "hold fast the form of sound words" (II Tim. 1:13). He further taught that as a minister,

Romans 1:11-12 gives an illustration of the kind of fellowship that Paul enjoyed with other believers. How does his description of this activity differ from our modern concept? Have you ever enjoyed fellowship in the sense that Paul describes in these verses?

Think About It!

Timothy had the responsibility not only to teach sound doctrine himself but also to ensure that the next generation was preserved from error: "The things that thou hast heard of me among many witnesses, the same commit thou to faithful men, who shall be able to teach others also" (II Tim. 2:2). These "faithful men" were to be measured by a number of criteria. One prerequisite that Paul established for ordaining a man to the ministry was that he be "apt to teach" (I Tim. 3:2). This qualification seems to be an allusion to a special spiritual gift. To serve as a shepherd over parts of God's flock, men must have received from Christ's Spirit the supernatural enabling to be "pastors and teachers" (Rom 12:7; I Cor. 12:28; Eph. 4:11).

Successful ministry of the Word is, of course, a two-way street. The most-gifted, best-trained minister cannot change a believer's life. To grow spiritually, believers must receive the Word preached or taught and submit to it. James addresses this need when he exhorts his readers, "Be ye doers of the word, and not hearers only, deceiving your own selves. . . . Whoso looketh into the perfect law of liberty, and continueth therein, he being not a forgetful hearer, but a doer of the work, this man shall be blessed in his deed" (James 1:22, 25).

Fellowship

Although not all of us are able to minister the Word publicly, we are all gifted for the spiritual labor of fellowship. It is appropriate to refer to this activity as a spiritual labor because, contrary to popular usage, biblical fellowship is essentially spiritual, and it is work. Our English word *fellowship* does not express the same force that the Greek word communicates. The Greek word, *koinonia* (koi noe NEE uh), refers to a mutually beneficial activity that two or more people enjoy because of something they have in common. To coin a phrase, *koinonia* is "in commonship."

In the Bible's presentation of the church, *koinonia* can describe the labor of meeting each other's needs through the operation of the spiritual gifts believers possess by the Holy Spirit. By teaching one another, giving to meet physical needs, conversing about our great God, or testifying to God's working in our lives, we offer to the brethren blessings that mutually edify because of our common enjoyment of the indwelling Spirit. Such spiritual interaction does not have as its ultimate purpose coming to know one another better. Ultimately, *koinonia* serves the purpose of knowing *God* better. As the apostle John implied in his testimony, "That which we have seen and heard declare we unto you, that ye also may have fellowship with us: and truly our fellowship is with the Father, and with his Son Jesus Christ" (I John 1:3).

Ordinances

Before leaving this earth, our Lord commanded that two rites be practiced in His church. He established baptism as the initiatory rite that is to announce the entrance of a new believer into the body of Christ (Matt. 28:19). The night of His betrayal, He instructed that one part of His final meal with the disciples be observed regularly in the meetings of the church (Luke 22:14-20; I Cor. 11:17-34). Any of us who have attended church regularly are familiar with the practice of these ordinances. However, without some effort to understand what the Bible teaches about them, we will fall into the trap of formalism—adhering to the outward form of these rites but not appreciating their meaning. If we want to enjoy the spiritual benefits that God intends to give us through these ordinances, we must come to understand their significance.

Baptism

Although coming to Christ in salvation is a hidden work that no human can see, Jesus Christ has no "secret followers." He once told a group of Jews, "Whosoever shall be ashamed of me and of my words, of him shall the Son of man be ashamed, when he shall come in his own glory" (Luke 9:26). For this reason our Lord instituted a ceremony that would serve as a public proclamation of God's hidden work in the heart of a believer. When a person is regenerated, God somehow unites that believer with Christ in His death, burial, and resurrection and thus gives him new life (Rom. 6:1-11). When that believer is baptized, he publicly declares through the symbol of immersion that he believes Jesus Christ was buried and raised for him and that God has indeed united him with His Son.

One question that has troubled theologians and laymen alike for centuries is the question of whom to baptize. Should the church baptize the infant children of believing parents, or should it baptize only those who have professed faith in Christ themselves. Those who favor infant baptism usually base their position on two observations. First, they state that since certain New Testament passages refer to entire households being baptized (Acts 16:15, 33; I Cor. 1:16), the Bible evidently teaches that infants are to be baptized. Second, they observe that since baptism replaces circumcision as the new initiatory rite for the community of God's people (Col. 2:11-12), it must be that little children should be included as subjects of baptism.

What Would You Say?

Many professing Christians believe that baptism is a necessary means of salvation. This belief is called *baptismal regeneration,* and the following verses are often used as key proof texts for this idea: Mark 16:16; Acts 2:38; Romans 6:1-11; and I Peter 3:21. How would you account for these verses?

It seems, however, that both of these observations form very weak arguments. The passages that mention entire households being baptized never state that infants were part of those households. And every subject for baptism that is specifically identified in Scripture was a person old enough to understand the gospel and trust Christ for himself. The second observation is also problematic. It fails to recognize the difference between Israel and the church. Paul explained that the church was not Israel, but rather was to be understood as "one new man" (Eph. 2:15). One way in which these two institutions differ is that whereas Israel was a nation, the church is a called-out community of faith. Since people became members of Israel by being born to Israelite parents, it was only natural that the initiatory rite in the Old Testament should have infants as its subjects. However, people enter the church by repenting and believing the gospel for themselves. Therefore, it seems only logical that the subjects of this rite should be different from those in Old Testament Israel. The proper subjects of Christian baptism should be only those who have chosen to trust Christ for salvation.

Through the observance of baptism the Lord richly blesses His people. The person being baptized enjoys a physical experience symbolic of God's spiritual work in his soul. Just as his spirit was mysteriously buried with Christ and resurrected with Him to new life, so his body is submerged in water and raised again in triumph. It is also a visible expression of that person's public identification with Christ as His disciple and of his commitment to follow Christ. But perhaps the greatest blessing is for those of us who watch. Not only are we privileged to see Christ's church expand by the unashamed profession of another convert, but we are also reminded of our own riches in Christ. Like the person being baptized, we have been united with Christ, and therefore we can be confident that we are forgiven, enjoy an intimate relationship with God through His Son, and possess the ability to live a new life victorious over sin.

The Lord's Supper

From the beginning of the Christian church, believers have obeyed the Lord's command to reenact regularly one part of His final meal with His disciples—the eating of the bread and drinking

of the cup (Acts 2:42; I Cor. 11:17-34). During that supper Christ explained that the bread was to symbolize His body, which was broken for all believers (I Cor. 11:24). Later He revealed that the cup they drank from represented the new testament, or covenant, that the shedding of His blood would effect on Calvary's cross (v. 25). The new covenant that He referred to was most likely the new covenant that God spoke of in Jeremiah 31:31-34. This passage mentions several particulars of

a covenant that differs significantly from the covenant that God gave through Moses. The essential provision of this new covenant is forgiveness: "I will forgive their iniquity, and I will remember their sin no more" (Jer. 31:34). All the other provisions are simply results of this one central element. Whereas the laws of the Mosaic covenant told people of God's expectations and underscored their failure to meet those expectations, the new covenant of Jeremiah promised full and free forgiveness. This forgiveness, our Lord taught the night before His death, is possible because of the shedding of His blood.

The purpose of observing this ordinance can be expressed in one word—*remembrance*. Christ instructed, "This do in remembrance of me" (Luke 22:19; I Cor. 11:24). What particularly we are to remember about Christ is revealed in the two elements, the bread and the cup. As we eat the bread, we are to remember that Christ's work for us came at great personal loss. His body had to be broken. Knowing how easily and quickly we forget, the Lord Jesus has given His church a regular physical reminder in the form of broken bread pieces. Just as an assembly physically benefits from a single loaf of bread because it has been broken in many pieces, so God's church spiritually benefits from the riches of Christ only because His body was torn and broken for each of us. Meditating on our Lord's agonizing death should turn our hearts to Him in thankful prayers and fill our souls with sublime wonder. As Charles Wesley penned, "Amazing love! how can it be/ That Thou, my God, shouldst die for me." This meditation should also challenge us in our commitment to the Lord. Peter reveals that one reason Christ suffered was to show us that suffering is part of being a follower of God: "Christ also suffered for us, leaving us an example, that ye should follow his steps" (I Pet. 2:21). Those that have followed Christ in His suffering steps know that suffering is necessary to knowing the Lord truly. It was one of

Paul's most important goals in life: "That I may know him, and the power of his resurrection, and the fellowship of his sufferings" (Phil. 3:10).

We are also to remember our Lord by drinking the cup. Just as we easily forget how costly our redemption was for the Lord, so we are also prone to forget the simplicity of our salvation. The new covenant that provides forgiveness for all our sins is accomplished through no good work of our own. Our forgiveness lies entirely in the blood of Jesus. As we partake of the cup, we should remind ourselves that the blood of Christ alone is sufficient to save our souls. We should also remember that a fresh cleansing from that blood is available at any time to reunite us into full fellowship with God: "The blood of Jesus Christ his Son cleanseth us from all sin" (I John 1:7).

Prayer

Returning to our snapshot of the early church (Acts 2:42), we discover that prayer is another essential duty of Christ's body: "And they continued stedfastly in the apostles' doctrine and fellowship, and in breaking of bread, and in prayers." Jesus Christ revealed the night before His crucifixion that one reason He was returning to His Father was to facilitate a new liberty in prayer for the church that He would soon found: "He that believeth on me, the works that I do shall he do also; and greater works than these shall he do; because I go unto my Father. And whatsoever ye shall ask in my name, that will I do" (John 14:12-13). This promise is fundamental to the successful operation of the body of Christ. The church is not armed with physical weapons for its growth. Its goals and its powers are spiritual, not physical. Nevertheless,

PRAYING

BIBLICALLY

Scripture contains many exemplary prayers, which are recorded to help us learn to truly pray in Jesus' name. The following is a list of some of the most famous prayers in the New Testament:

The Lord's Prayer—Matthew 6:9-13
Christ's High-Priestly Prayer—John 17
The Apostles' Prayer in Persecution—Acts 4:24-30
Paul's Prayer for Spiritual Understanding—
Ephesians 1:15-23
Paul's Prayer for Power—Ephesians 3:14-21

143

it does conquer in the physical realm because of the spiritual work of prayer. And Christ's promise regarding the effectiveness of this work is staggering: "If ye shall ask any thing in my name, I will do it" (John 14:14).

We should notice, however, that the same assurance that gives us remarkable liberty in prayer also limits us. Christ has not promised to answer any prayer—only those prayed in His name. Certainly, His promise does not refer to all prayers that happen to have "in Jesus' name" perfunctorily attached. Our Lord's usage of this phrase should be taken as parallel to its usage in John 14:26, where Jesus assures His disciples that the Father would send the Holy Spirit "in my name." Since the Father sent His Spirit to minister in the place of Jesus on earth, we should understand Christ's promise as applying to prayers prayed as Christ would pray—they are supplications so in keeping with Christ's person and work that He Himself could make them before the Father.

I would like a bicycle and computer. Please remember your promise to me in John 14:13.

In Jesus' name

Since this qualification rules out many of the prayers we pray regularly, some may complain that it seems to nullify the promise. However, when one considers all that Christ would pray, one begins to realize the glorious magnitude of the Lord's promise. We can pray in Christ's name for the grace necessary to love the brethren truly (John 13:34), for the obedience to have our joy full in Christ (John 15:11), for the growth necessary to see Christ's body attain the "measure of the stature of the fulness of Christ" (Eph. 4:13), and for the prospering of the gospel so that the ends of the earth are evangelized (Acts 1:8).

Paul recognized the amazing supernatural power that members of Christ's body have available to them in prayer. For this reason his epistles are filled with excerpts from his prayers for the saints—all of them composed of requests that can be confidently prayed in Christ's name. In those letters Paul also frequently pleads with believers to intercede with God for him in his ministry. In the conclusion to his epistle to the Romans, Paul's request for prayer becomes impassioned: "Now I beseech you, brethren, for the Lord Jesus Christ's sake, and for the love of the Spirit, that ye strive together with me in your prayers to God for me" (Rom. 15:30). Paul had come to learn a lesson that all of us likewise must learn. The greatest edifying work that we can do for other members of Christ's body is to intercede for their spiritual growth and success.

Music

Even a cursory review of church history demonstrates that the church of Jesus Christ is a singing church. This interest in musical expression has not come from some vain fascination with emotionalism. It is the result of a biblical mandate (Eph. 5:19; Col. 3:16). Music has played a dominant role in the church from its founding because God has ordered it to be so, and He has given His people specific instructions regarding this music's purpose and content.

Purpose of the Church's Music

God intends that the music of His people accomplish a spiritual work. Music in Christ's body is not entertainment, and it is not to be viewed as a "time-filler" for its public meetings. Music is one important way that the Holy Spirit uses believers to accomplish His work within God's holy temple. For this reason, Paul speaks of music as a direct result of the Spirit's filling: "Be filled with the Spirit; speaking to yourselves in psalms and hymns and spiritual songs" (Eph. 5:18-19). Specifically, music serves the purpose of edifying the saints. Those who minister musically must not think of themselves as performers; they are teachers and exhorters: "Teaching and admonishing one another in psalms and hymns and spiritual songs" (Col. 3:16). Music is also to serve the purpose of praising God. We are to "teach and admonish" each other with our music, but in it all we should be "singing with grace in our hearts *to the Lord*" (Col. 3:16; emphasis added).

Paul expands on this theme in his instruction to the Ephesians: "Singing and making melody in your heart to the Lord; giving thanks always for all things unto God and the Father in the name of our Lord Jesus Christ" (Eph. 5:19-20). When we sing songs of worship in our services, we must remember that our audience is not the saints surrounding us in the pews. We are the living stones of a glorious temple, and in our presence is the almighty God, invisible but enthroned (I Cor. 5:4; Eph. 2:20-22).

Content of the Church's Music

Paul's words in Ephesians 5:19 and Colossians 3:16 guide believers in their understanding of God's expectations for the content of their music. The music of the church must be biblically accurate. In Colossians 3:16, the

phrase, "Singing with grace in your hearts to the Lord" expresses one means of fulfilling the command "Let the word of Christ dwell in you richly." Of course, if our music is not biblically correct, it will hinder us from giving the Word a rich dwelling in our hearts. It should not be surprising, therefore, that in both Ephesians and Colossians, the first kind of music that Paul says believers should use is "psalms." In previous generations of the Christian church, the Book of Psalms played a central role in the music of believers. Now, however, it is rare for most assemblies of God's people to use even one psalm set to music in a week of services. Nevertheless, God's Word is clear, "Speaking to yourselves *in psalms*" (Eph. 5:19; emphasis added).

Paul also states that the church should use "hymns." These are pieces of music that express praise to God. Such songs address the Lord directly or indirectly and give thanks to Him for what He has done or for what He is. "Praise Ye the Lord, the Almighty" and "For the Beauty of the Earth" would be two examples of a hymn. The third kind of music that Paul commands is "spiritual songs." This general phrase governs all church music that is neither a psalm nor a hymn. Usually, these are songs that are intended to encourage believers by testifying to God's goodness in daily Christian experience. Songs such as "It Is Well with My Soul" and "No One Ever Cared for Me Like Jesus" probably fit into Paul's category of "spiritual songs."

Conclusion

As we conclude our consideration of ecclesiology, and all of theology, it is appropriate for us to meditate on the privilege of being the recipients of divine revelation. In His final discourse with His disciples, our Lord revealed, "Henceforth I call you not servants; for the servant knoweth not what his lord doeth: but I have called you friends; for all things that I have heard of my Father I have made known unto you" (John 15:15). Revelation alone, of course, does not make one a friend of God. As Christ Himself said in that final address, revelation must be obeyed for one truly to be a friend of God: "Ye are my friends, *if ye do whatsoever I command you*" (v. 14; emphasis added). What did our Lord command those first members of His church? "These things I command you, that ye love one another" (v. 17). In a sense, all of our study of God and His ways points us back to one word—*love*.

We have learned about God (His attributes and His works), man, Jesus Christ, salvation, and the church. But all of this valuable information is useless to us unless we use it to love God more fully and love others more sacrificially, for on these two loves "hang all the law and the prophets" (Matt. 22:37, 40). As Paul said, "Though I have the gift of prophecy, and understand all mysteries, and all knowledge; and though I have all faith, so that I could remove mountains, and have not charity [love], I am nothing" (I Cor. 13:2). If, however, we make love our goal, our study will come to life, guiding us through this life and preparing us for the one to come—a life ruled by our Savior, "Him that loved us, and washed us from our sins in his own blood" (Rev. 1:5).

Blest Be the Tie

John Fawcett, 1740-1817

Blest be the tie that binds
Our hearts in Christian love;
The fellowship of kindred minds
Is like to that above.

Before our Father's throne
We pour our ardent prayers;
Our fears, our hopes, our aims are one,
Our comforts and our cares.

We share our mutual woes,
Our mutual burdens bear;
And often for each other flows
The sympathizing tear.

When we asunder part,
It gives us inward pain;
But we shall still be joined in heart,
And hope to meet again.